Creative Leadership: How to Motivate and Inspire the Designers, Content Creators, and Writers on Your Team

K. Lee Butler

Published by Sailfish Features, 2024.

CREATIVE LEADERSHIP: HOW TO MOTIVATE AND INSPIRE THE DESIGNERS, CONTENT CREATORS, AND WRITERS ON YOUR TEAM

First edition. September 19, 2024.

Copyright © 2024 K. Lee Butler.

ISBN: 979-8224786671

Written by K. Lee Butler.

Table of Contents

Foreword

So leading a team of creative individuals is tougher than you thought it would be? Over the centuries, countless managers and leaders have been blindsided by the reality that leading artists is infinitely harder than leading other non-creative employees. Welcome to this study on Creative Leadership. It is a resource designed for those who lead teams of graphic designers, videographers, writers, musicians, and all other forms of creative professionals. If you have picked up this book, then you have likely encountered the unique challenges of managing a team that thrives on the expression of creativity. But don't worry. I am here to guide you through the complexities of creative leadership. In this book, we will explore the fundamentals of leading creative teams, including how to effectively communicate, inspire, and collaborate with your team. Additionally, we will delve into the importance of understanding and nurturing your team's creative processes, as well as how to navigate the potential conflicts and obstacles that may arise.

So buckle up and get ready to expand your leadership skills in the realm of creativity. Together, we will unlock the full potential of your team and pave the way for successful and innovative projects. Let's begin!

Notes for Getting Started

I had a title in mind for this book: "How to Lead Like Your Creative Team's Future Hangs on Your Success." But since it was a bit of a mouthful, I have chosen to forgo that title. However, I want you to know that our focus will not be on "How to Lead Like Your Future Hangs on Your Success." Don't misunderstand - your future is important and should be a priority. But, the most effective leaders are those who prioritize the futures of their team members above their own. Remember this perspective as you read, as it will provide the context for all the tips and ideas presented in this book. Leaders with a self-centered approach will likely gain little from its contents.

If you strive to become the kind of leader who leaves a lasting impact on your employees; if you aspire to be the leader who is praised in an acceptance speech by a then former team member twenty years from now; if you aim to lead a team that remains intact and content for decades because no one wants to leave - then this book is for you.

A crucial point to note: This book delves into the intricacies of leading creative teams. The traditional management skills that may have proven successful for you in the business sector or in the military are unlikely to suffice in a creative team environment. Why, you may ask? Because creative individuals possess unique wiring and perspectives. They often have strong egos and an innate need for validation. As leaders, it is imperative to foster trust and create a culture of psychological safety where team members feel empowered to share their ideas, even if they deviate from the norm, without fear of judgment or ridicule. Furthermore, one must keep in mind that there are typically fewer opportunities for growth and advancement within creative career paths. As such, it is not uncommon to find oneself in a position of leading a team comprised of individuals twenty years one's senior who have amassed significantly more experience and knowledge over the years.

All of the leadership lessons contained within these pages have been gleaned from my personal experiences (or from the experiences of close colleagues and friends). The individuals who have played a role in these stories shall remain unnamed, their identities protected to avoid any harm or embarrassment. For over two decades, I have been at the helm of creative teams - guiding and supporting them - witnessing firsthand how they can either flourish or falter based on the quality of their leadership.

Let's Get This Concern Out of the Way First

Before diving into the practical advice presented in this manual, I want to address a potential concern that may arise for some readers. It is understandable some (particularly those from more analytical career backgrounds) may worry that following these tips could lead to laziness or entitlement among their creative team members. I want to point out that this book does not touch upon issues of recruitment and hiring. That is a delicate topic on its own. Instead, this book assumes that you have already assembled an exceptional team of dedicated individuals with strong work ethics. When collaborating with passionate and driven creatives, it is imperative to offer them a level of independence. Creatives have a unique approach to doing work, which may differ from the approaches of traditional employees. That is, in fact, probably why you decided to pick up this book! You've discovered that leading creative teams isn't quite the same as leading other groups of employees. I'm here to help you develop a leadership approach that works for your uniquely-wired team.

Ready to Start?

Through trial and error, I have learned some hard lessons as I watched some of my own teams crumble due to my mistakes as a leader. But looking back, I realize that great leadership is not something reserved for an exclusive group of individuals. It is not rocket science; it is a skill that anyone can develop and possess. Yes, anyone. There is no person who lacks the potential to become an inspiring leader, one who rallies and motivates creative employees and leads his team towards success.

It is not about having the perfect degree in business management or extensive experience. It is not even dependent on having exceptional team members working under you. Rather, it is about being self-aware, cultivating positive habits, and honing effective communication skills.

But above all, it is about earning the trust and loyalty of your creative team by showing them that you always have their best interests at heart - no matter what challenges may arise. And the key to achieving this lies in shifting your focus from yourself to your team; putting their needs and goals above your own. By doing so, you are already halfway towards becoming an outstanding leader that your team will appreciate and value.

Chapter 1: Leading in a Quiet Quit Culture

———

During my time working on a reasonably large-scale marketing project, I was partnered with a young branding and communications specialist named Amy. For privacy reasons, all names in this story (and subsequent stories) have been changed. Alongside myself, there were two other colleagues on our team: a highly experienced woman named Jean and our project manager Kara. Every day, Amy poured her heart and soul into the project. She exuded qualities of diligence, intelligence, and bold forward motion. It was evident that she had aspirations of advancing quickly into a leadership role.

Unfortunately, our fearless leader Kara hit a personal roadblock and had to step down from the project. This presented an opportunity for Amy to make a power move as she continued to excel in her work.

However, just when things seemed to be falling into place for Amy's rise to the top, the company made an unexpected decision. They brought in an external candidate, Paul, to take over Kara's position. With his impressive resume boasting ex-military experience and relevant skills, it seemed like a match made in heaven for our team. As I perused Paul's LinkedIn page, I couldn't help but feel starstruck. How could we possibly go wrong?

The Mistakes

On Paul's first day as our team leader, he gave a motivational speech expressing his enthusiasm for leading us. As part of the introductions, he distributed copies of his dazzling resume as a way for us to get to know him. Soon enough, Paul made **Mistake #1:** He revealed that he saw our project as a valuable addition to his portfolio. It was as if he had told us that we were just supporting characters in his career story.

It's important to remember that Paul had a background in the military. He was used to following orders without question and was unaccustomed to being asked about why something needed to be done. When he joined our team, he immediately took charge and completely revamped the project we had been working on for six months. Any suggestions or concerns from our team were met with a fierce defense from Paul - he could have been a lawyer with his skills. In a matter of weeks, our team's hard work was erased and replaced with Paul's ideas. Our protests fell on deaf ears and expressions of concern were ignored. It was made clear that Paul was the sole creator of this project, and we were merely his support staff.

I vividly remember when Amy expressed her frustration to him. She had dedicated so much time and effort into the project, only to have it all wiped away. But he didn't see the issue. "Why is this a problem?" he asked innocently. "I didn't think your work would impress the client, so I gave you direction on how to fix it."

That was three mistakes in one statement.

Mistake #2. Paul demonstrated that he didn't take Amy's concerns seriously and that he couldn't be reasoned with.

Mistake #3. Paul assumed that being a leader meant solely solving the team's issues and delegating tasks for others to execute.

Mistake #4. Paul let a creative employee know that he didn't think her unique creative style was all that great.

For those who are unaware, Mistake #4 is deadly. It's a one-shot kill - from friendly fire, no less. If you are caught holding the smoking gun, your team may lose all trust in you. Beware of showing any doubt in a creative's professional abilities or unique style. Only reveal such concerns if you have a valid reason to let that person go, and only if you actually have the authority to do so.

But before we move on, let's revisit Mistake #1: Paul revealed that he saw our project as an opportunity to enhance his portfolio.

Mistake #1. *Paul revealed that he saw our project as a valuable addition to his portfolio.*

Been to any good concerts lately? Watching a rockstar perform is always a thrilling experience. But as the old saying goes, "Never meet your heroes." This is especially true for those who know that many rockstars can be difficult to work with. They often have a sense of entitlement and expect others to cater to their needs. While this mentality may bring short-term success, it is damaging in the long run for both the team and the client.

As Paul learned, focusing solely on personal success and disregarding the needs of his team and the client can lead to resentment and frustration. A great leader puts his team's growth and success above his own and knows how to effectively communicate to keep everyone on the same page and empower them to do their best work. In contrast, a rockstar only cares about himself and will eventually alienate his team members. So if you're leading a creative team, focus on being a leader rather than a rockstar.

Mistake #2. *Paul's disregard for Amy's concerns demonstrated that he could not easily be reasoned with.*

Think back to a time when you tried to get assistance from someone who had no interest in helping you. Perhaps it was a call to customer support, a visit to the DMV, or even talking to a friend or family member. Remember how that person's lack of empathy made you react.

Did you persist in trying to get her to understand, despite knowing that your efforts were futile? More likely than not, you quickly realized the conversation was pointless and walked away - at least for the moment. The person you were speaking with probably thought she had won the argument by shutting you down. But did you ever go back to her for help again? Or did you just return to the DMV the next day and purposefully choose another line?

This concept extends to leadership as well. If a team member agrees to follow your direction with a simple "Fine, we'll do it your way," it doesn't necessarily mean he is fully on board with your idea. You have simply persuaded him to act in accordance with your plan for the time being; he may still hold reservations about your strategy. And if a seasoned creative professional is not fully committed to the project, then why are you working with him at all? The company could have easily hired an entry-level assistant to transcribe your ideas at a much lower cost.

A Better Approach

In order to avoid making Mistake #2, Paul should have stayed quiet and listened attentively to Amy until she had finished speaking. If they were in a group setting, he could have suggested moving the conversation to a more private space to allow them both to save face if necessary. Even if Amy takes a break from speaking, Paul should continue asking questions and seeking clarification to encourage her to share more. The ultimate goal is for Amy to express all of her thoughts and concerns before ending the conversation.

While Amy speaks, Paul should refrain from formulating his own responses or arguments; instead, he should actively listen and demonstrate his full engagement in the discussion. After Amy has finished sharing (without rushing), Paul may feel inclined to respond immediately, but it would be best for him to hold off. Instead, he could say something like, "Thank you for bringing your concerns to my attention, Amy. I want to make sure I take this issue seriously and explore all potential solutions before reaching a conclusion. Can we schedule another meeting for tomorrow at 10:00 a.m.?" This gives Paul time to gather his thoughts and prevent himself from saying anything he might regret.

During this time, he should come up with 3-5 practical solutions that address Amy's concerns. When they reconvene the next day, Paul can present these options to Amy and allow her to choose the one that she believes is the best fit. This approach gives her a sense of control and responsibility, which can lead to genuine loyalty towards both Paul and his ideas.

Mistake #3. *Paul believed that being a leader meant solving all of the team's issues and then dictating the solution for the team members to carry out.*

Effective leaders expect their team to be capable of tackling new challenges and stepping up when needed. If a team member becomes accustomed to simply shutting off her thinking and relying on the leader to solve all issues, it can hinder her development. In this scenario, the leader is enabling mindlessness in the team member.

Let's take a brief moment to pause and reflect on this. In my experience, most good employees are eager to actively participate and contribute in their work. Think back to when you worked with a recent graduate in her first job - did she immediately come to you for answers when faced with a problem or difficulty? Most likely not. She probably tried to figure it out on her own, even if she made some missteps along the way. Similarly, remember when you were with a young child whose shoelace came untied - if you attempted to help him, chances are he would insist on doing it himself.

When an employee stops bringing his own solutions to the table, it's usually because his natural inclination to think through and solve problems has been suppressed. As a leader, you have the authority to either encourage or discourage proactive thinking in your employees. If you consistently dismiss or criticize your team members' ideas and solutions, eventually they will stop sharing them with you.

I understand that sometimes you genuinely believe your solution is the best one. And perhaps it is. But whenever possible, allow your team members to come up with their own solutions, even if it may not be as perfect as yours. The important thing is that you are teaching them to think independently and proactively. With time, their problem-solving abilities will improve.

Think Deeper

As a manager, it's easy to get caught up in constantly dealing with urgent issues. It can feel like playing the game "whack-a-mole" at a carnival, where moles keep popping up and you have to hit them down with a mallet. As soon as you hit one mole, another one pops up. Work-related problems can be similar, demanding your attention one after another, and you want to solve them quickly so you can move on to the next challenge. But as a team leader, your main focus should not be playing whack-a-mole; instead, it should be on developing your team and creating a strong dynamic where everyone works together towards a common goal. This means delegating problem-solving tasks to your team members so that you can focus on building a cohesive and successful team.

A Better Approach

If Paul had understood this concept beforehand, he could have avoided causing Amy's frustrations altogether. If he had noticed any specific problems with her report, he should have discussed them with her directly and sought out her ideas for potential solutions. Instead of addressing the issues, he instead made changes to the entire report without explaining what he saw as problematic. Then, he instructed Amy to implement his solutions without involving her in the decision-making process. This approach left her wondering, "What was wrong with my original work?" and "Does Paul not have faith in my abilities?".

Mistake #4. *Paul made the mistake of expressing his disappointment with an employee's unique creative style.*

Never do that. Even if you think her creative look and feel is trash, keep it to yourself. Creative team members have a distinct perspective when it comes to their careers, unlike other employees. They understand the value of their unique styles and voices and how it sets them apart. If their boss doesn't appreciate their approaches or tones, they may risk losing their jobs. Unlike an accountant's work, which is focused on precision and accuracy, an artist's work is subjective - her individual style and ideas are on full display for all to see and critique. This constant pressure can lead to a fear of job security when receiving criticism from those in higher positions.

Let's take a closer look at this situation. We are all aware that creative work is highly subjective, and what one person finds appealing may not appeal to another. Even if industry research supports a certain style or approach, the decision-maker's personal preferences can ultimately determine the success of a project.

In this particular case, Amy's thought process was, "Kara hired me because she appreciated my unique style. But she's gone and this new person doesn't seem to like it as much. Maybe I should start looking for a new job so I can leave on my own terms before I get dropped." Not only did Paul jeopardize Amy's job security by making her fear his disapproval of her style, tone, and voice - he also created uncertainty among the rest of the team about their own roles. If Paul was willing to criticize the star performer (whom everyone else on the team had praised until now), what chance did the rest of us have?

While Paul probably didn't intend any harm with his comment about the client not liking Amy's work (and may have only said it to deflect questions or criticism), he has now taken on the responsibility of managing a group of anxious creatives.

A Better Approach

Here's what Paul should have done. The right way to handle the issue of job security starts with Paul making a pact with himself that his employees will never know about. The pact goes something like this:

"As a responsible leader, I will always prioritize valuing my creative team members as individuals who, like all other team members, have families to support, children to educate, and mortgages to pay. I will never let go of a member of my creative team for personal taste or stylistic reasons. Instead, I will work with her over time to make her style the signature of our company. My main responsibility is to my team, not just achieving my own preference."

You may be wondering, "Wait a minute - why can't the creative team member just adapt her style to match mine?" But think about it this way. That team member's unique creative style, much like your own personality, has been developed and refined over a significant period of time. Your personality is shaped by both inherent traits (such as being introverted or extroverted) and environmental factors during your formative years. Additionally, you have likely read books, educated yourself, and honed your skills to excel in certain areas. All of these elements work together to make up who you are as a person. So can you simply change your personality and show up at a meeting with a completely different version of yourself? Not likely.

If you have the chance to choose your own creative team members from the start, that's ideal. This allows you to establish the company's style right away. However, if you inherit a pre-existing team and are responsible for keeping them together, making significant changes may not be an option. As a leader, your main duty is to guide and support the team as it currently stands.

Think Deeper

Lastly, I want to emphasize that as a leader, your main responsibility is to the team as a whole, and not to individual team members. If there is someone who is causing harm or disrupting the team's dynamic, it is your duty to protect the group and allow any necessary consequences for that person, even if those consequences may be difficult or uncomfortable for him to experience.

A Better Approach

In this scenario, Paul could have used phrases such as the following:

- "I know all this is subjective, but I prefer..."

- "This is fantastic work. I can tell you've been doing this a long time. Because of the client's preference for... might I suggest..."

- I love your style. Can we maintain this overall tone and feel while trying it with more of a blue color palette and a sans serif font?

The final statement is effective because it provides concrete instructions for the team member to follow. It's frustrating for an artist to hear, "I just don't like it. Try again." What specifically don't you like? Is it the font, color, imagery, or text itself? Break it down for the artist and give him a clear path forward.

To avoid Mistake #4, Paul should have provided a greater sense of security for his team. This does not mean making false promises about tomorrow - no one can predict the future. But as a manager, there are small ways to make team members feel secure. For instance, assigning a team member to lead a meeting can show that her development as a future leader is important to you. Recommending training materials for another team member can also demonstrate investment in his growth. These gestures show employees that they are valued and that you as the leader want them to stay with the company. When an employee is encouraged to learn new skills that benefit the team, it sends the message that his boss sees potential in him, thus increasing his motivation and dedication.

After outlining Paul's four main leadership mistakes, let us revisit the story of how his management style clashed with Amy's goals. It was during our third week together that I heard a particular phrase slip from Amy's lips. My heart sank as soon as I heard it; I knew there would be problems for our team. Paul had approached Amy for her thoughts on a change he wanted her to implement (purely out of courtesy, of course, not because he valued her input). "Do you agree with that?" he inquired.

Amy's response? "I don't care."

"I don't care" – words no leader ever wants to hear. Something was clearly wrong. How did Amy, who had once poured so much time and passion into this project, suddenly lose interest and stop caring? She had given up. Quiet quitting had taken over.

If you're not familiar with the term "quiet quitting," it describes employees who are disengaged and unproductive, only completing the bare minimum required in their jobs without taking on any additional tasks or volunteering for projects. This behavior is unacceptable and can indicate unhappiness or disinterest in one's job, leading to negative effects on productivity and overall morale.

Let me be clear - quietly quitting is essentially stealing from your company by accepting a paycheck for work that you aren't fully invested in. If you find yourself reduced to nothing more than a "typist," simply transcribing your boss's thoughts without any real contribution, then at least have the courage to speak up to HR and suggest finding a more fulfilling professional opportunity. And leaders, if one of your employees ever does this, it will reflect poorly on you. Though quiet quitting is a clearly unacceptable practice, it is almost always a sign of an unfulfilling and meaningless workplace culture... and the responsibility for this failure falls on the leader.

Over time, our creative team went from constantly communicating updates, sharing personal achievements and struggles, and offering encouragement, to barely speaking to one another. Our wings were clipped, our confidence shattered, and our ambition extinguished. Paul found himself dragging a dead weight across the finish line, wondering how he had come to lead what seemed like the world's worst creative team - ironically, one that he himself had shaped.

Summary

In hindsight, Paul's initial error was transparently disclosing his true agenda to the team: he had joined solely to advance his own career rather than to support the team or client. This made it obvious that the project would benefit him and no one else. His second blunder was being obstinate and refusing to consider any suggestions that contradicted his plan. Consequently, the team stopped sharing their insights and concerns with him, creating a "just tell us what to do" mentality. With his third mistake, Paul seized control of the problem-solving process, leaving no space for creativity or growth within the team. Lastly, by voicing disdain for a team member's work and creative style, Paul fostered a tense and skittish working environment.

Each of these errors contributed to a breakdown in synergy within the team. Instead of working together with motivation and ambition, we became a demoralized and disconnected group of individuals simply trying to fulfill our job responsibilities. Ultimately, all of these mistakes stem from one central theme: Paul prioritized his own personal success over the success of his team. The lesson here is that if you are only interested in your own growth and advancement, leadership may not be the right role for you. A true leader's primary duty is to serve his team.

Chapter 2: The Times They Are A-Changin'

The year was 1984. George, a driven entrepreneur with a passion for video production and advertising, joined forces with a small-town marketing firm. The business owner was open-minded and mentored George, teaching him valuable skills in the industry. When the owner retired a decade later, George stepped up as President of the company. He had a gift for attracting clients and excelled at communication and building interpersonal relationships. However, his love for videography never waned.

As time passed and technology advanced, George's marketing agency flourished. He began contemplating adding an in-house video production service to their offerings. This is when he met Mark, an enthusiastic videographer who applied for a position at the firm. At only 25 years old, Mark showed great potential from his experience working for a prominent brand's internal marketing team after graduating. His peers admired his creativity and exceptional work ethic, and George saw his talent immediately.

George offered Mark the chance to head up the new video production department at the agency. This role would involve liaising with clients, coordinating shoots, and overseeing projects from beginning to end. Although Mark already handled these responsibilities in his current job, he was thrilled at the prospect of building a video department from scratch at a thriving firm. He eagerly accepted the position, even taking a pay cut as he believed that establishing a successful video division within an already prosperous agency would lead to future financial gains and earn him the eventual title of "Project Manager".

On Mark's first day, he was taken by surprise when George handed him a stack of flyers. "Anytime you aren't busy making a video, you'll need these to hand out during your sales calls."

Sales calls? And by "calls"... did we mean knocking on doors, as in "the salesman came a-callin'?" Mark was horrified. No one had said a word about sales during the interview. He was terrible at sales.

George had bumbled into **Mistake #5**. George had assumed that Mark would be okay with doing an undiscussed task just because everyone else on staff did it too. From George's point of view, sales is an essential part of working at a small agency. It's just something that everyone has to do. But for Mark, the idea of being responsible for sales made him uneasy - he didn't feel like it was his strong suit. On his first day of work, Mark's confidence wavered and he started to question if he had accepted the job offer too quickly.

As time went on, the agency received its very first request for a video project from a client. Mark was thrilled, but George was absolutely elated. He had been waiting 30 years for the opportunity to use his passion for video production in a professional setting. Just as Mark sat down to begin responding to the inquiry, George burst into the office with excitement and announced that he had already taken care of it. "Don't worry about responding - I have all the details and notes ready," George exclaimed.

Although Mark didn't say it out loud, he couldn't help but think to himself, "That's unfortunate. I wanted to establish myself as the main point of contact for this project." As George placed a stack of handwritten notes on Mark's desk, Mark realized that not only had George responded to the inquiry, but he had also already had a phone call with the client. Mark couldn't help but wonder why he wasn't included in that important conversation. This brings us to **Mistake #6**.

George was so passionate about the project that he jumped right in and forgot all about Mark's involvement.

Mark came to the meeting with the client fully prepared, equipped with relevant questions, budget guidelines, and a portfolio showcasing his project boards and look books. However, he was caught off guard when George unexpectedly announced that he would also be attending. Despite being designated as the point of contact for the client, Mark struggled to get a word in edgewise as George eagerly took charge and presented his own ideas. In the end, the client agreed to whatever George suggested. The next day, Mark found a script on his desk for a commercial they would be shooting, making him wonder why he wasn't consulted as the script-writer. On the day of production, George had already packed up the company car and was ready to go before Mark even arrived (despite Mark's usual punctuality). It became clear to Mark that George had no intention of giving him any significant role in the shoot; instead, he was relegated to holding the boom pole while George controlled the camera. As a result, the client assumed Mark was just an intern for the semester.

Throughout the editing process, George loomed over Mark's shoulder, nitpicking every cut and edit. He dictated precisely where to trim each clip, down to the exact frame. George also personally selected the background music and instructed Mark on the placement of text graphics, which font to use, and what color scheme to follow. Mark was becoming increasingly exasperated with George's meddling and the final product began to look like something straight out of a 1980s time capsule. Yet, George was having so much fun that Mark didn't want to ruin his enthusiasm. Plus, the client had given his stamp of approval for "whatever George thought was best." As soon as it hit 5 o'clock, Mark left for home while George stayed behind to finish his own work that he hadn't even looked at all day due to his preoccupation with micromanaging the video project.

Here we find **Mistake #7**. George failed to delegate tasks to Mark and instead got too involved in the project. He fell into the trap of wanting to participate in the more exciting aspects of the job. Is video production enjoyable? Of course. But it was Mark's responsibility to handle video production-related tasks. He was brought on board to communicate with clients, assess their needs, and make recommendations. Mark was supposed to produce and direct the videos and make editing decisions. However, throughout the entire process, he did none of those things.

Five years passed, and each project was identical to the last. Clients started to realize that every commercial produced by the agency was a recycled idea, causing project requests to decline. Mark grew increasingly bored with his work. He realized that the only way to maintain his skills was to find and work on personal video projects, even if they were unpaid. Whenever someone offered an opportunity for a "videographer to gain experience", Mark eagerly volunteered. He believed that practicing and improving his skills without pay was better than sitting around doing nothing while waiting for George to come in for an editing session. Despite his hopes of one day leading a video project at work, it never came to fruition. George began to resent seeing Mark's unpaid work being done during working hours. And Mark resented George's decision to turn his role as a Video Project Manager into a part-time salesperson and part-time production assistant.

After five years, Mark finally discovered what he considered to be George's **Mistake #8**. While the company continued to grow and evolve, George had no interest in modernizing his video production techniques or adapting his leadership style. He remained adamant about using the same camera, setups, methods, and styles from years ago. Despite Mark's attempts to suggest changes and progress, George clung to the status quo.

One day, Mark was bored at work and decided to clean out an old equipment closet. In the process, he stumbled upon a pile of outdated video production gear. This discovery led Mark to realize that George's attachment to the video production division stemmed more from nostalgia than a willingness to embrace new methods and processes. It became clear that George's unwillingness to adapt would prevent any real growth or progress within the company. As a result, Mark began updating his resume and wished he had done so sooner.

The Mistakes

Mistake #5. *George assumed that everyone on staff at the small marketing firm was responsible for sales, and therefore Mark would have no issue taking on the task.*

However, Mark had no reason to expect this responsibility unless it was clearly stated in his job description in writing. As a result, he not only lacked the necessary sales skills to perform well, but also felt deceived and mistrustful of his manager, George. This situation highlighted the importance of clear communication and setting realistic expectations from the beginning. While George did not intentionally deceive Mark, his failure to clarify the full scope of the role led to unnecessary tension between them. It served as a lesson learned about the dangers of making assumptions without proper clarification.

Furthermore, George should have discussed his hands-on involvement in video productions and his personal direction of all projects to avoid any misunderstandings. He should have set realistic growth expectations for Mark within the company instead of giving him false hope that he could significantly impact the success of the agency's video department.

During Mark's interview, George exaggerated the company's capabilities, leading Mark to believe he was joining an established organization with a solid client base. He also made it seem like Mark would be in charge of the video production division. Upon starting the job, Mark realized it was more of an assistant role. If George had been transparent about the less appealing parts of the position, Mark could have made a more educated decision about joining the company.

Mistake #6. *George allowed his passion for videography to interfere with his responsibilities as a leader.*

There's no denying that creativity is fun. For those who spend their days confined to a desk, the opportunity to bring ideas to life visually is like a breath of fresh air. This is especially true for aspiring writers and avid movie buffs...the chance to create a television commercial must have been an exhilarating experience.

However, George's excitement got the best of him. As stated by Newton's first law of motion, objects will maintain their current state of rest or movement unless acted upon by an external force. Once George got some momentum working on a project that truly ignited his passion, he couldn't seem to stop. This is a common occurrence for creatives; it often starts in college when they are given their first real creative class projects. They stay up all night working on those glorious masterpieces... and then sleep through their algebra exams. As creatives gain more experience and advance in their careers, they must learn how to control and channel their creative energy effectively.

George's excitement for his first video project in years caused him to pick up too much momentum. This led Mark to lose his own motivation to impress clients, knowing that George would just step in and take over the work anyway. As a result, George developed a belief that Mark was incompetent and could never handle the role without him, leading to a self-fulfilling prophecy where Mark was seen as a "useless assistant." Over time, Mark's skills and mindset deteriorated due to lack of use, because George neglected his main responsibility as a leader: to support and empower his team members for success.

Mistake #7. *George's inability to delegate tasks resulted in him being overworked, while his staff members were bored.*

Bored creative team members usually create trouble. If you fail to keep a creative team member engaged in worthwhile projects, he will likely seek out other tasks to occupy his time, like Mark did when he began taking on unpaid assignments that he knew his boss wouldn't care to be involved in. However, the work he finds may not align with your own goals.

Working dogs are truly remarkable creatures. Whether they are herding livestock, searching for missing persons, assisting individuals with disabilities, or detecting suspicious items at airports, their abilities are unmatched. However, trainers stress the importance of giving these intelligent dogs a meaningful job to do in order to prevent destructive behaviors. Without proper stimulation, they may resort to chewing furniture or shoes. Similarly, creative team members thrive when given consistently challenging and meaningful tasks that allow them to showcase their talents. While there may be times when mundane assignments are necessary, regularly giving one creative individual these types of tasks can communicate a lack of trust in his abilities. Just like an unsatisfied puppy will find ways to occupy its time when left alone, a frustrated and bored member of a creative team will likely find projects that interest him - whether the rest of the team wants him to or not.

Mistake #8. *George's disinterest in updated industry trends and techniques undermined Mark's trust in the company's capabilities to deliver a great product.*

During sales meetings, Mark sometimes found himself recommending other local video production companies instead of his own. He was well-aware of that his reputation hung on his recommendations, and did not want to risk it by suggesting a service that did not meet a client's needs.

Furthermore, in a small town like theirs, Mark knew how crucial it was to maintain good relationships with competitors. He wasn't willing to poach other agency's clients or burn any bridges - after all, he might be relying on one of those competitors for a job someday! While George may have viewed Mark's mindset as disloyal, Mark was simply being practical. He saw that George's company was struggling and knew he needed to plan for his own future employment. Mark was not content with staying in the same position without any opportunities for growth. It just wasn't feasible for him to do so.

If George had thought about it, he would have realized that of course Mark must either advance or move on. ...But the status quo is often comfortable, isn't it?

...One last note regarding George's Mistake #8. His tendency to live in the past impacted not only his technical skills, but also his leadership style.

In the beginning of his career, George had to handle everything himself out of necessity; he was essentially a one-man marketing team. However, as the company grew and new team members were added, George should have shifted his focus from doing tasks to delegating and coordinating them. Unfortunately, George failed to adapt his leadership approach, which ultimately hindered the company's overall growth.

Think about what would happen if you continued to parent your children using the same techniques that you used when they were toddlers as they grew into teenagers or young adults. They would become emotionally and mentally stunted, wouldn't they? Likewise, it is essential for leaders to adjust their strategies as their businesses go through various stages of growth.

George approached business management as if it were a recipe to follow - the idea being that if he followed the same process over and over again, everything would turn out fine each time. But in reality, leading a creative team during periods of growth is more like raising a child. It's crucial to adapt your strategy as the team progresses through different stages of development.

Summary

I want to take a moment to address Mark's significant error throughout this process. He was too passive and did not ask enough questions during the job interview. He also neglected to obtain a written schedule of future salary increases based on performance, as well as a clear list of his job responsibilities. Instead of speaking up about George's micromanagement, Mark stayed silent and let valuable time slip away without taking any action. Both Mark and George were unaware of how much time had passed until it was too late. George held onto outdated beliefs about professional standards, while Mark struggled in his subsequent job search due to having little to show for the past five years of his career. Both would have been wise to consider the words of Bob Dylan: "The times they are a-changin.'"

Chapter 3: The "Pantser"

———

You writers know what I'm talking about. Some of you are "Pantsers". That's right. You fly by the seat of your pants every day. No outline, no timeline, no structure. And what's crazier? You actually think this lifestyle is kind of fun. The rush of an impending deadline. The thrill of risk. Like an adrenaline junky, you get a sort of spike out of the last-second emergency turn-around.

Well, the rest of us think you're bonkers. It doesn't matter if you've become the head honcho, or if you're still an intern... it's time to stop being a "Pantser".

I was once hired by a "Pantser", a project manager named Ronald who was known for his lack of organization and last-minute scrambling. At the kickoff meeting, we participated in team-building exercises and introductions while Ronald gave an inspiring speech about our potential to secure future work with the client if we successfully completed this project. Go team.

We'd go our separate ways, and begin working on our assignments. Weeks would pass. The team never heard from Ronald. We knew he had other projects on his plate, so we initially gave him the benefit of the doubt. However, as the deadline approached and we still hadn't heard from him, our nerves began to grow. Despite our best efforts to reach out and share our progress with him, Ronald seemed to have disappeared.

About a week prior to the deadline, we would finally get in touch with Ronald, only to be met with criticism and blame for not following his instructions (which were often vague and barely communicated). Ronald had "explicitly said" to do this or that - (he used that phrase a lot, and it usually meant that the thought had once crossed his mind, and we should have been well aware of it). So why hadn't we done it? Panic would set in as we scrambled to make major changes to a massive project in record time.

Because we realized that we were short on time - and that Ronald would still need to proof our edits - we worked fast. Within two days, we'd have our revisions completed and submitted for Ronald's review. And then?

...You guessed it. Crickets. Ronald was gone again. Golfing? Beach day? No one knew. But wherever he was, he didn't seem to be very stressed about the huge deadline that was now only days away.

The day before the hard deadline, Ronald would finally take a look at our revised work. Without fail, he would call us around 4:00 PM with a newfound idea that just came to him. He was convinced that this idea would revolutionize our project and demanded we incorporate it somehow. The first time this happened, we went above and beyond to make his last-minute vision come true. But after the second time, we began learning to push back and tell him no. By the third incident, we were all quite comfortable with standing up to Ronald and refusing his demands. Of course, he would then stay up all night working on "our" project (as he thought it), while congratulating himself for single-handedly completing such a massive task while his team went home to rest.

Ronald was a "Pantser", someone who flew by the seat of his pants without much planning or consideration. His mistakes cost him the respect and trust of his team members.

The Mistakes

Mistake #9. *Ronald was too "hands off" in the early stages of the project.*

You might protest, "But the ability to delegate is a crucial hallmark of a growing leader!" The ability to delegate is indeed essential for growth, and yet there are countless leaders who have not yet mastered this skill. (George in Chapter 2 serves as a prime example.) But the true act of delegation entails more than simply handing over tasks; it involves releasing responsibility and relinquishing control. Had Ronald delegated responsibility for the project at hand, he would have also given away his right to any last-minute ideas or changes. And yet, it was clear that Ronald still wanted to retain his involvement in the project. Thus, he should have made an effort to remain actively present from Day 1, rather than stepping back and delegating tasks without fully committing himself to the project's success.

A Better Approach

Ronald's desire to maintain his involvement in the project was apparent from the start. However, he failed to fully immerse himself in the project, choosing instead to remain distant and detached from the group. Had he made a conscious effort to actively participate and communicate with his team on a daily basis, he could have ensured that his expectations were clear from the very beginning. Additionally, setting aside dedicated time each day to personally review the progress of the project and align it with his goals would have greatly contributed to its success. Unfortunately, Ronald's lack of consistent involvement ultimately hindered rather than aided the project's progress.

Think Deeper

A true leader's unwavering presence is the lifeblood of a thriving creative team. Ronald could have been the catalyst for innovation, inspiring and motivating his members to reach their full potential. Instead, he adopted a passive attitude, simply hoping for success without actively working towards it. This approach is flawed for several reasons. Firstly, a creative team will never fully trust a leader who isn't fully invested in their journey. A leader must not only physically be with his team, but also mentally and emotionally engaged. He must be able to empathize with their team's struggles and guide them towards success.

In addition to preventing potential trust issues, there are many other important reasons why a leader should regularly and consistently engage with his team during a project:

- **Effective Communication.** When a leader is regularly involved with his team, it fosters trust and encourages open communication. Team members are more likely to share their ideas and concerns when they feel that their leader is actively listening and engaged.

- **Aligned Goals.** Consistent involvement from a leader helps to ensure that the team is working towards the same overall objectives. By actively participating, leaders can clarify expectations and address any misunderstandings.

- **Conflict Resolution.** In any creative project, conflicts are bound to arise. A leader's presence can help mediate these conflicts, find common ground, and keep the team focused on achieving the end goal.

- **Overcoming Challenges.** Creative processes often come with challenges and obstacles. Whether it's discovering a lack of necessary resources or software, a leader who is intimately involved can identify potential issues early on and provide solutions in a timely manner.

- **Maintaining Quality.** A leader's perspective can offer valuable insights into the direction of the project. Regular involvement allows the leader to ensure that the work aligns with both the project goals and the target audience's needs.

- **Resource Management.** With a good understanding of the creative process, leaders can effectively allocate resources to ensure that the team has everything they need for success.

- **Decision Making.** Important decisions are often made throughout the creative process. A leader who stays involved can make sure these decisions are made promptly and strategically for the benefit of the project.

Mistake #10. *Ronald had poor communication skills.*

I quickly picked up on the fact that Ronald had a tendency to use metaphors in his speech. While I appreciate a clever metaphor, there are certain situations where direct and clear instructions are more appropriate. Effective communicators understand when to use creative language and when to be straightforward, and they always make sure that their messages are understood correctly (often by confirming multiple times).

Ronald was known for his frequent use of the phrase, "I explicitly said...". In his mind, his metaphors and word pictures were clear instructions that could easily be acted upon. However, to the rest of the team, his directives were often vague and subject to interpretation.

It is crucial to consider direction as actionable information. I once had the pleasure of working with an exceptional director who truly understood creative leadership. He would often jokingly tell our team, "Just give me the same thing. Only better." He was well aware that in the real world, creatives are constantly given direction like this. But he also recognized how absurd and impossible those words actually were.

"Give me a really eye-catching image that makes people want to buy our product."

When a creative is given a project with vague instructions like the one above, she knows it will be a challenging task. The creative may be curious about what exactly the client means by "eye-catching" and what the target audience is looking for in a product. A better approach would be to provide clear guidelines, such as: "Design a square Instagram post for women aged 32 to 40. Use bright colors and bold fonts, but avoid green as the client does not prefer it. Recommended fonts are Adobe Sirenia and Glodok. Include an image of a mother and child smiling at a park with a playground in the background. Use the provided header text and captions." This direction is clear, actionable, and difficult to misinterpret.

The Importance of Providing Actionable Feedback

I want to stop here for a moment on this idea of prioritizing actionable feedback. A key component of successful leadership is the ability to solicit, receive, and implement constructive feedback. Yes - I went there. Not only should a leader be able to solicit solid, constructive feedback... he also should be capable of receiving it. Not everyone has the grace to do so.

Let's dive into some tips that should be incorporated into your leadership strategy for a creative team:

1. Create a Culture of Open Communication

- **Encourage honest dialogue.** Establish a safe and supportive environment where team members feel comfortable sharing their thoughts, ideas, and concerns without fear of judgment or reprisal.

- **Active listening.** Demonstrate genuine interest in the feedback provided by your team members. Pay attention to their words, tones, and body language to gain a deeper understanding of their perspectives.

- **Regular check-ins.** Schedule regular one-on-one meetings or team discussions to provide opportunities for feedback exchange. This can help to maintain open lines of communication and address issues promptly.

2. Analyze Feedback Objectively

- **Identify patterns.** Look for recurring themes or trends in the feedback received. This can help to pinpoint areas where the team may be struggling or excelling.

- **Separate emotions from facts.** Avoid making assumptions or jumping to conclusions based on emotional feedback. Focus on the underlying issues and concerns.

3. Develop Action Plans

- **Prioritize feedback.** Determine which feedback items are most critical and require immediate attention.

- **Create specific goals.** Set clear and measurable goals based on the feedback received.

- **Assign responsibilities.** Assign tasks and deadlines to team members to ensure accountability.

- **Monitor progress.** Track the progress of the action plans and make adjustments as needed.

4. Provide Constructive Feedback

- **Be specific.** When providing feedback, be clear and concise. Avoid vague or general statements.

- **Focus on specific actions.** Rather than criticizing the person or the overall product, focus on specific actions that need to be taken to achieve the desired outcome.

- **Offer suggestions.** Provide constructive suggestions for improvement.

- **Be open to feedback.** Be willing to receive feedback from your team members as well. This demonstrates your commitment to open communication and continuous improvement.

Interestingly, the one time that I had the opportunity to share with Ronald that I needed clear, actionable feedback from him in order to successfully complete a project, he gave me the most honest response I've ever received from a boss. Ronald said, "I don't want to give you actionable feedback because I know that if I do, and I still don't like the end result, you'll just say that you followed my instructions. I don't want to take on that sort of responsibility." Aha. Perfect honesty.

The answer I gave him? "You *are the leader*, Ronald. That makes you responsible. We are a team. I am on your side. If you don't like the result of your direction, you *should* take responsibility for it. But remember - it's not the end of the world. We'll just try again."

Mistake #11. *Ronald expected his team members' minds to work the same way that his did.*

While he may be capable of having fresh ideas for a project at 3am the day before it's due, most people can't work that way. Not only that, but he also imagined that his team members might have the exact same creative ideas that he was having, and somehow telepathically translate his ideas into writing. It doesn't work that way. If you leave a creative alone to do a job, she will implement *her* ideas. If you want *your* ideas to be implemented, be ready to spend a few hours spelling those concepts out in great detail, using actionable language.

The chapter highlights a common pitfall in leadership: assuming that one's own mental processes are universally shared by others. This assumption, often rooted in a combination of overconfidence and a lack of empathy, can lead to significant misunderstandings and inefficiencies within a team.

Ronald expected his team members to operate in a manner that aligned perfectly with his own work habits. He viewed his ability to generate fresh ideas at the eleventh hour as a standard, rather than an exception. He overlooked the diverse ways in which individuals approach tasks and manage time. While some may thrive under pressure, others require a more structured and planned approach. By assuming that everyone works like him, Ronald set unrealistic expectations that led to frustration, burnout, and a decrease in productivity.

Furthermore, his belief that his team members might somehow telepathically understand his creative ideas backfired. As discussed in the previous section, creativity is a highly personal and subjective process. What may be immediately clear to the leader may still be entirely ambiguous to others. Effective communication requires explicit and detailed explanations to ensure that everyone is on the same page. Ronald assumed a shared understanding of his preferences, but what he ultimately got was the team's interpretation of his ambiguous direction.

A Better Approach

While it may be tempting to simply delegate tasks and expect the desired outcome, effective leadership involves providing clear guidance, offering support, and actively monitoring progress. By spelling out concepts in great detail, the leader ensures that there is no room for misinterpretation and that his team members are equipped with the necessary information to complete tasks successfully.

Ronald would have benefitted from a more empathetic and collaborative approach. Here are some strategies to consider:

- **Open Communication.** Encourage open dialogue and feedback from team members. This will help you as the leader understand your team members' perspectives, work styles, and potential challenges.

- **Active Listening.** Practice active listening to truly understand the thoughts and ideas of team members. This involves paying attention, asking clarifying questions, and showing genuine interest.

- **Empathy.** Put yourself in your team members' shoes and try to see things from their perspectives. This can help you understand their motivations, concerns, and limitations.

Setting Clear Expectations

While it's important to be flexible and understanding, it's also essential to set clear expectations. This will help ensure that everyone is on the same page and working towards a common goal.

- **Define Goals and Objectives.** Clearly articulate the project's goals and objectives, ensuring that everyone understands his role in achieving them.

- **Provide Guidelines and Deadlines.** Establish clear guidelines and deadlines, but be open to adjustments based on individual circumstances or unforeseen challenges.

- **Offer Support and Guidance.** Provide ongoing support and guidance to help team members stay on track and overcome obstacles.

By adopting a more empathetic, collaborative, and supportive approach, you as a creative leader can create a positive and productive work environment where team members feel valued, empowered, and motivated to achieve their best.

The Power of Predictability

In the final section of this chapter, there is one crucial concept that I hope to impart. It's the power of predictability. We've all heard the saying, "Marry an accountant...not an airline pilot." (Not that there's anything wrong with airline pilots, of course.) But it speaks to a deeper understanding - the wisdom in seeking out stability and predictability.

Humans, as creatures of habit, find comfort and security in predictability. While spontaneity can be thrilling, there's also great value in knowing what to expect. Predictability can alleviate stress, foster trust, and give us a sense of control over our lives. Whether it's a consistent daily routine, a dependable partner, or a reliable income, the power of predictability lies in its ability to ground us and provide stability.

As a leader, you have the opportunity to give your team this gift. Be a predictable leader - one who can provide a steady foundation for your team to build upon and grow from. In doing so, you will create a sense of trust and security within your team, allowing them to thrive and reach their full potential.

Summary

Let's part ways with the "Pantser" leadership style, in favor of the more effective "Planner" leadership style. A Planner leader is one who values early involvement, effective communication, and planning ahead to avoid last-minute changes. This style promotes a sense of trust and security within the team, as well as clear expectations and guidelines for achieving project goals.

In summary, this chapter highlights the importance of early involvement, effective communication, goal setting, empathy, and predictability in successful leadership. These qualities not only benefit the project outcome but also create a positive work environment where team members can thrive and reach their full potential.

Chapter 4: The Over-Committed Leader

A close associate of mine confided in me about a job experience he had faced in the past. He joined a company with strong visionary goals, which was rapidly expanding. He was brought on board to fill an immediate vacancy as a project manager, responsible for communicating with clients, evaluating their requirements, and assigning tasks to team members who would handle the actual work. Essentially, his role centered on ensuring client satisfaction.

It didn't take long for my friend to see that the company was growing faster than its employees could keep up. Even with the thrill of working in such a fast-paced environment, problems soon surfaced. The team he was tasked with managing was constantly swamped, trying to meet high demands with limited resources. Tight deadlines led to a decline in the quality of their work. My friend found himself stuck between pleasing clients and recognizing the limitations of his team.

As weeks slid into months, it became apparent that the strain was not sustainable. Projects were delayed, clients became increasingly frustrated, and his superiors were less than supportive when he approached them with these issues. The company's vision seemed to be clouded by its ambition for growth, overlooking the welfare and satisfaction of both its employees and clients.

A recurring issue my friend encountered was that during meetings, company executives would make grand promises to clients without considering the feasibility or budget constraints. Initially, the clients were thrilled by these promises and their expectations skyrocketed. However, my friend had to later meet with these clients in private (away from the company management's ears) and explain that the promises made were unrealistic. In order to fulfill them, the clients would need to increase their budgets.

The Mistakes

Mistake #12. *The company's leadership was driven by creative dream-casting, but at the expense of realistic planning and business management.*

In other words, the company's vision was "all vibes, and no plot." The phrase "all vibes, and no plot" became a running joke among the project team, but as the weeks wore on, it became a painful reality to confront. My friend's initial excitement for the project began to dwindle as he came to realize the stark disconnection between the executives' visions and the harsh realities of the project. It was more than just an inconvenience; it was a structural flaw that threatened to unravel all their hard work.

As each unrealistic promise piled up, a wall of mistrust grew taller and thicker between the clients and the team. One afternoon, during a particularly tense conference call with a major client who had been continually disappointed by unfulfilled promises, my friend found himself delicately navigating through an increasingly treacherous situation. The client's frustration spilled out, recounting how their expectations had been consistently let down and how this pattern could no longer be overlooked. My friend apologized profusely, desperately trying to salvage what he could by offering alternative solutions, but the damage had already been done—a deep-seated rift now existed between the clients and the team.

Determined to address the recurring issues plaguing his job, he scheduled a meeting with his superiors. With a sense of urgency and frustration, he prepared a detailed presentation that illustrated the significant gap between promises and deliverables using real project examples and client feedback. He proposed a bold new framework for client communications—one that involved key project members from the start and required executive promises to be cross-checked with those who would ultimately be responsible for implementing them.

Despite initial signs of agreement in the meeting, nothing changed the next day. The same old cycle continued—promises made without consulting the team about feasibility within existing time, manpower, and budget constraints.

My friend found himself caught between an immovable rock and an unyielding hard place. He tried multiple times to reason with upper management, but it became clear that leaving the company was the only practical solution to this ongoing issue. And so, the company lost a valuable and highly skilled employee that day.

A Better Approach

After he resigned, my friend took some time to reflect on his experiences and began to sketch out what a better approach might have looked like, both for him and the company. He understood that growth was essential, but it should not come at the cost of the company's integrity or the quality of its deliverables.

He envisioned a strategy where communication was paramount, not just between the client and the project manager but all tiers of the company. This included regular, structured updates involving all stakeholders where everyone was on the same page about what was feasible within given constraints.

My friend suggested that in an ideal world, before any promise was made to a client, there would be a preliminary internal meeting with the key project members to discuss the feasibility of the client's demands. Here, resource availability, budget limits, and realistic timelines would be thoroughly vetted before making any commitments.

Mistake #13. *The company's leadership had failed to anticipate growth and its accompanying challenges.*

I once had the opportunity to work with an independent film company, whose website boldly displayed a list of corporate values. One such value, prominently highlighted, read: "Prepare for rain." The foundation for this concept was drawn from a small yet powerful film called "Facing the Giants". Within it lay a story about two farmers, both struggling through a season of drought. Desperately wishing for rain to fall upon their land and bring life to their crops, they prayed fervently for a miracle.

One farmer, filled with hesitation and doubt, retreated back inside his home and rationalized, "I cannot afford to waste my seeds by planting them now. If and when I see rain clouds forming, then I will start sowing." The other farmer, however, had unwavering faith that God would send rain and immediately set out to plant his field. When the storm finally arrived, it came with surprising force and speed. The farmer who had waited found himself unable to plant his seeds in time, and thus missed his chance. But the faithful farmer who had planted his seeds ahead of time was prepared for the downpour. As a result, his crops flourished and he reaped a bountiful harvest.

In the case of my friend's workplace, the management may have *wanted* growth. They may have even *prayed for* growth and taken steps toward *pursuing* growth. But they failed to structurally prepare their company for growth to occur. This glaring oversight led to a cascade of operational breakdowns. As pressure mounted, the company's infrastructure, which was barely adequate at its previous size, began buckling under the weight of increased demands. The team was trying to perform large-scope projects using systems and processes that had been designed for small budgets and limited resources.

As the company continued to grasp at larger contracts and expand its client base without adjusting its internal mechanisms, the strain began manifesting not only in project delays but also in employee turnover. Talented individuals who, like my friend, could no longer align their professional integrities with the chaotic trajectory of the company, started to leave. This turnover further exacerbated the problem, as training new employees while trying to deliver on overly ambitious projects became an additional hurdle.

The leadership's response to these escalating issues was to push even harder for growth, viewing it as the only way to outpace their problems. They adopted a "grow at all costs" mentality which only deepened the foundational cracks. Team meetings became sessions of firefighting strategies rather than constructive planning discussions. The morale of the team hit an all-time low as they felt their concerns were ignored and their professional capabilities pushed beyond reasonable limits without proper support or acknowledgment. The result was not just dissatisfied clients or overworked staff, but a slow erosion of the company's once stellar reputation.

A Better Approach

The company's leadership would have done well to pause the acceptance of new clients for a season as they developed an implementation plan for scaling the company more strategically. This plan would include not only an upgrade of internal systems and processes to handle larger projects but also a comprehensive training program aimed at aligning new and existing employees with the company's updated operational goals and constraints. Additionally, a robust feedback system should be established, enabling real-time communication between all levels of the company hierarchy. This would ensure that both challenges and suggestions could be addressed promptly and effectively.

In revising their approach to client relations, the leadership could introduce a phased commitment strategy. Under this plan, initial client meetings would serve as exploratory sessions to understand fully the client's needs and expectations. Following this, a detailed proposal would be drafted, outlining phased deliverables which would be reviewed and approved internally before any commitment is communicated to the client. This would not only manage clients' expectations more effectively but also ensure that the company's promises are always aligned with its capabilities.

Mistake #14. *The team was severely under-staffed.*

Closely related to Mistake #13, this mistake can stem from a number of different factors. The biggest that I will discuss here is that often, leaders of creative teams fail to account for human error in their division of manpower and resources. They tend to plan based on the ideal scenario where every team member is operating at 100% capacity, without considering the complications of sick days, personal emergencies, or even the inevitable ebb and flow of creative energy. This oversight can lead to a workforce that is spread too thin, which not only dampens productivity but also affects the overall quality of work and employee morale.

This could be observed in how projects were allocated among the team. With each person already juggling multiple responsibilities, any unforeseen complication in one project could cause a domino effect, putting additional stress on other projects and team members. Most troubling was that this situation frequently led to projects being rushed to completion, compromising the quality that the company was known for.

A Better Approach

The better approach would involve a more realistic assessment of resource allocation. This assessment would account for potential roadblocks and ensure that each project has a buffer—additional manpower or time set aside to handle unexpected issues. Moreover, regular reviews of workload distribution should be conducted to prevent burnout and maintain high standards in deliverables.

Mistake #15. *There was a lack of investment in continuous professional development.*

Driven by the relentless desire to expand and tackle new ventures, the company had overlooked a vital aspect - keeping the team's skills aligned with current industry standards and emerging technologies. The neglect of investing in professional development resulted in a gradual decline in competitiveness among the workforce, while the disparity between their capabilities and the demands of intricate projects continued to widen. As a result, client satisfaction dwindled as the team grappled with outdated skills to meet modern requirements. It was a predictable outcome, like trying to fit a square peg into a round hole, as the company failed to keep pace with evolving trends and advancements in their field.

A Better Approach

As a company striving to lead its industry, the pursuit of continuous professional development should be woven into its very fabric. This entails regularly scheduled training sessions, hands-on workshops, and access to cutting-edge courses that keep the team on the forefront of emerging trends and technologies. A dedicated budget specifically allocated for professional growth would demonstrate the company's commitment and prioritize the importance of ongoing education in their annual operational plans.

With these proactive measures in place, employees will not only feel valued and empowered in their roles but also equipped with the necessary skills to confidently tackle complex projects. Thus, fostering a culture of continuous learning directly contributes to heightened productivity and an elevated level of client satisfaction.

Summary

In summary, these three mistakes made by the leadership at my friend's prior workplace highlight the importance of thoughtful planning, resource allocation, and organizational adaptation in the face of growth. Leadership must integrate strategic foresight with operational reality to ensure that the company not only grows but does so sustainably. This includes preparing for potential challenges, understanding the limits of current resources, and investing in both the infrastructure and the team to meet future demands.

The responsibility of leadership is not just to chase opportunities for growth but to also steward the resources—including human capital—that make growth possible and sustainable.

Chapter 5: It All Trickles Down From the Top

The issue of poor leadership at the executive level causing widespread dissatisfaction within a company is a common problem. It is difficult for me to choose just one example to share, as I have encountered many cases like this in my career. However, there is one particular client that stands out in my mind. He owned a small event production company and could only be described as a five-year-old in an adult's body. He was known for his embarrassing temper tantrums and his knack for pushing his employees to their limits every day. His behavior created a company culture of fear and instability, as he was rude, demanding, and impulsive. It was almost as if he lived in his own fantasy world - one where he was admired and worshipped by all. Little did he know, the respect quickly dissipated the moment he left the room. I remember a time when, during a marketing call, one of his employees quipped (in private, of course), "I have a new motto for our company: 'Miserable People Delivering Misery Directly to You.'" This was a satirical take on the company's current motto, and it elicited applause and laughter from everyone on the call who found solace in knowing they were all suffering together.

While the jest brought a moment of camaraderie and relief among the team, it also sparked a shared realization: something needed to change. As expected, employees began to depart. Within the company, there was a group of co-workers who regularly shared job opportunities and encouraged another to submit applications. They would say things like, "Maybe this is your chance to break free from here. I hope you make it."

The company's high turnover rate was a direct result of the owner's poor leadership. He had a habit of making impulsive decisions without consulting his team, causing chaos and confusion within the organization. His lack of communication skills also led to misunderstandings and mistakes, which further contributed to the dissatisfaction among employees.

Moreover, the owner's behavior affected not only his employees but also his clients. Due to his constant mood swings and unprofessional conduct, the company lost several important contracts and gained a negative reputation in the industry. This resulted in financial losses for the company, leading to layoffs and an even more toxic work environment.

Despite numerous complaints from his team and evidence of his poor leadership, the owner refused to acknowledge any wrongdoing or make any changes. He believed that he was always right and that everyone else was just trying to bring him down. This arrogance and disrespect towards his employees only added fuel to the fire. The employees were overworked, demotivated, and constantly living in fear of their boss's outbursts. Morale was at an all-time low as people dreaded coming into work each day.

This experience taught me firsthand how one bad leader at the top can ruin an entire company's culture. It also emphasized the importance of effective leadership skills in creating a positive work environment where employees feel valued, motivated, and respected.

The Mistakes

Mistake #16. *The company's owner chose not to invest in strengthening his own emotional intelligence.*

As the saying goes, "People don't leave jobs, they leave managers." In my experience, this statement holds true. Many employees can withstand long hours, difficult tasks, and even lower salaries if they have a supportive and understanding leader. Unfortunately, the opposite is also valid. One bad manager can ruin an entire team's motivation and drive for their work.

Take a moment to pause and consider... Just as leaders who openly struggle with self-control issues should work to improve their emotional intelligence, so too should every individual. It is a valuable skill that can be nurtured and honed by anyone, regardless of his background or current level of personal growth. There is endless potential for expanding self-awareness and gaining a deeper understanding of one's emotions. The journey towards emotional intelligence has no limits, and there is always room for further development and advancement.

Emotional Intelligence

Defined as the ability to understand and manage one's emotions while recognizing and influencing the emotions of others, emotional intelligence (EI) plays a significant role in how leaders interact with their teams.

According to research by TalentSmart, 90% of top performers have high EI, while only 20% of bottom performers do. Additionally, companies that focus on hiring and developing emotionally intelligent leaders have a 34% higher return on investment than those who don't.

Why is emotional intelligence so crucial in leadership? Let's take a closer look at some of its essential elements:

Self Awareness. Self-awareness is the cornerstone of emotional intelligence. It involves recognizing and understanding one's own emotions, strengths, weaknesses, values, and goals. Leaders with high emotional intelligence are aware of how their thoughts and feelings influence their behavior and decision-making.

On the contrary, a lack of self-awareness leads to blind spots that can hinder a leader's ability to empathize with his team members or recognize when his actions may be negatively impacting others.

In our case study, the owner lacked self-awareness. He never took responsibility for his aggressive outbursts or acknowledged the negative impact they had on his employees. If he had been more self-aware, he would have realized the need for better stress management techniques and he would have sought help with learning to control his temper.

Self-Regulation. Self-regulation is the ability to control one's emotions and impulses. Successful leaders possess this skill, and can keep their anger or excitement in check to avoid making hasty, reckless decisions. They carefully consider their actions and uphold a moral code that fosters trust within their teams. Additionally, they are adaptable and can handle change gracefully.

However, the owner of the event production company struggled with self-regulation. He often made impulsive decisions based on his current mood rather than on logical thinking or the welfare of his company. This unpredictable behavior not only bewildered his team but also weakened their confidence in his leadership, since they never knew how he would respond to challenges or feedback.

Empathy. Empathy is another core component of emotional intelligence that involves understanding and sharing the feelings of others. An empathetic leader can build deeper personal connections with team members, which enhances trust and loyalty. Additionally, empathy allows leaders to better understand client needs and provide more effective solutions.

Regrettably, the owner's lack of empathy was evident in his disregard for the emotional well-being of his employees and clients alike. His inability to perceive how deeply his actions affected those around him led to a hostile work environment and damaged relationships with clients, ultimately affecting the business's bottom line.

Social Skills. Lastly, emotional intelligence encompasses a set of social skills that enable leaders to build and maintain healthy relationships. These skills include effective communication, conflict resolution, persuasion, and team building. Emotionally intelligent leaders use these skills to foster a collaborative environment that encourages mutual respect and teamwork.

In the case of our event production company owner, his social skills were severely lacking. He communicated ineffectively with his team, often resorting to shouting and belittling rather than engaging in constructive dialogue. His approach to conflict was either to ignore it or to explode in anger, neither of which resolved the underlying issues. This failure to manage interpersonal dynamics contributed heavily to the toxic atmosphere within the company.

The culmination of these deficiencies in emotional intelligence had catastrophic effects on the company. As the owner continued to operate without self-awareness, self-regulation, empathy, or social skills, the workplace environment deteriorated further. The employees' morale plunged as they felt increasingly undervalued and misunderstood. This led not only to a high turnover rate but also to a decline in productivity and creativity among the staff who remained.

A Better Approach

It's important to recognize that emotional intelligence is a skill that can be developed and refined. Even if you currently lack confidence in this area, there are steps you can take to improve your emotional intelligence and become a leader who is respected and admired by those around you.

There is now a growing availability of training programs and workshops focused solely on developing emotional intelligence. These resources offer valuable tools for leaders seeking improvement, often including exercises that help individuals practice self-awareness, empathy, and effective communication skills.

Another effective method for enhancing emotional intelligence is through coaching or mentoring. A skilled mentor in EI can offer personalized guidance and feedback, pinpointing areas for improvement and providing strategies for growth. This one-on-one support can greatly aid in the development of a leader's emotional competency.

Regular feedback from employees also plays a crucial role in a leader's journey towards improved emotional intelligence. Encouraging an open dialogue where team members feel comfortable expressing their thoughts and feelings can bring to light aspects of a leader's style that may need adjustment. This feedback not only aids in personal development but also contributes to a culture of transparency and mutual respect within the team.

Finally, prioritize mental health and well-being. A leader who is stressed or burned out is less likely to exhibit high emotional intelligence. Regular exercise, sufficient sleep, and a balanced diet are all crucial for maintaining mental fitness and emotional resilience.

Mistake #17. *The owner of the company failed to receive and implement feedback from his team members.*

Had he established a regular system for receiving feedback, it would have opened up opportunities for him to understand the expectations of his employees. This failure to engage in a two-way communication process meant that many issues remained unresolved, brewing discontent amongst the staff.

By ignoring channels of feedback, the owner inadvertently isolated himself from his team's reality. His leadership, lacking in self-awareness and empathy, thus remained unchecked and uncorrected, steering the company towards operational inefficiency and a tarnished organizational reputation.

A Better Approach

One practical approach is to implement "360-degree feedback" sessions where not only does the manager evaluate the employee, but also the employee provides feedback to the manager. These sessions can be facilitated by an HR professional or an external consultant to ensure neutrality and effectiveness. Such opportunities not only aid in identifying areas of improvement but also help in acknowledging and reinforcing positive behaviors and practices.

Furthermore, these feedback sessions should be complemented with anonymous satisfaction surveys, giving employees a secure platform to express their true feelings without fear of reprisal. The aggregated data from these surveys provide leaders with clear insights into the overall climate of their organizations, pointing out trends and areas needing urgent attention.

Note: If a leader receives the same complaint from two individuals, it should raise a red flag. However, if that same grievance is echoed by three or more people, it is time for the leader to take action and address the issue at hand.

Mistake #18. *The owner of the company was emotionally unpredictable.*

This is a different sort of unpredictability than that found in the leader discussed in Chapter 3.

I have a passion for viewing director commentaries of movies. It's captivating to re-watch a beloved film and hear directly from the director about why he chose to convey specific emotions within a scene. One such commentary comes to mind when I think about the value of emotional predictability in interpersonal relationships.

While directing "The Chronicles of Narnia: The Lion, the Witch, and the Wardrobe", Andrew Adamson sought inspiration from the four children playing Peter, Susan, Edmond, and Lucy. In order to create the white witch's personality, he asked them about the most frightening characteristics they had noticed in some adults. Unanimously, the children agreed that *emotional unpredictability* was the trait that made some adults unbearable to be around. It's scary to not know how someone will react in certain situations!

As a leader, the owner of our example event company should have been the most stable and predictable person in the room. But instead, he allowed his own passions and whims to form his day-to-day decisions, resulting in a chaotic workflow. This unpredictability not only stunted the company's ability to develop structured, long-term plans, but also created a climate of uncertainty among the staff. Employees often found themselves at a loss, unable to anticipate the owner's reactions or understand the direction in which their projects were headed. This lack of consistency prevented them from feeling secure in their roles and diluted their sense of purpose within the company.

Consequently, as fear and confusion permeated the workplace, creativity and initiative began to wane. Team members hesitated to propose innovative ideas or take risks, for fear that an abrupt shift in mood or policy could render their efforts futile. The result was a stifling of growth that saw the company's offerings become less competitive in an industry where innovation is key.

A Better Approach

To counteract this harmful emotional unpredictability, the owner might have benefitted from implementing a structured decision-making process that included input from various team members. Establishing clear guidelines and criteria for making decisions would have helped to ensure that choices were consistent and aligned with the company's long-term goals.

Summary

In summary, the pitfalls faced by this company serve as a compelling case study on the importance of emotional intelligence in leadership. From failing to adequately handle feedback to allowing unpredictability to seep into decision-making, the missteps made were numerous and impactful. Each mistake highlighted throughout this analysis underscores a crucial aspect of leadership that was overlooked or mishandled.

Leaders must strive to develop their emotional intelligence to effectively manage both themselves and their relationships with others. By cultivating self-awareness, managing stress, being empathetic, improving communications, and maintaining a reliable approach in their professional conduct, leaders can foster a healthy, dynamic work environment that is conducive to productivity and creativity.

Furthermore, establishing regular feedback mechanisms, such as 360-degree evaluations and anonymous surveys, ensures continuous personal and organizational growth. These tools not only promote transparency but also encourage a culture of mutual respect and open communication. Additionally, structured decision-making processes can mitigate the risks associated with unpredictability and ensure steady progress towards organizational goals.

Leaders must strive to be the stabilizing force within their teams, providing clear direction and predictable responses that align with established principles and objectives. By doing so, they can create environments where creativity thrives, employees feel valued and respected, and ultimately, where organizations can achieve sustainable growth.

Chapter 6: Final Opportunities to "Get Better"

———

My sister-in-law, with her nerves of steel and the patience of Mother Teresa, took on the daunting task of teaching me how to ski. As we glided through the snowy slopes, she never allowed me to utter the words "I fell down". Instead, she encouraged me to say "I got better", thus turning every stumble into a learning opportunity. Likewise, the goal of this book reaches beyond highlighting mistakes; it aims to share these valuable learning experiences so that we may all "get better" at creative leadership. In the same way that my sister-in-law guided me down the mountain, this book will guide readers on the journey towards becoming successful leaders. Here are a few final opportunities to "get better" that I'd like to share with you.

Mistake #19: Becoming a Self-Appointed Leader

It was a few years ago when an eager social media manager, fresh out of college, joined our team. My first thought when I met her was that she reminded me of my younger self from twelve years prior - full of energy and ambition. My second thought was, "Oh, crap." Much like I had in my early days, she possessed natural leadership qualities, and she just couldn't wait to put them to use. She had taken it upon herself to lead the group as she aimed to step into the role of team manager - regardless of whether or not she was actually hired for the position.

I want to make it clear that while I support the development of leadership skills and expanding one's ability to lead, I do not advise appointing oneself as a team leader when not having been hired (officially) to do so. The reason for this is threefold.

Unclear roles and responsibilities can cause confusion and conflict within a team. This often leads to misunderstandings and tension among team members. To function smoothly, everyone must understand their places in the hierarchy.

Moreover, taking on a leadership role without official designation can undermine the authority of the designated leader. This can compromise the manager's effectiveness and disrupt team dynamics. Managers are chosen carefully, considering factors such as experience, skills, and team compatibility. Ignoring this process can create imbalance and resentment within the team.

Furthermore, assuming a leadership position without proper guidance can hinder one's professional growth. Eagerness to lead may overshadow the willingness to learn, which is crucial for career advancement.

The book of Proverbs offers wise advice on this subject: "Do not exalt yourself in the king's presence, and do not claim a place among his great men; it is better for him to say to you, "Come up here," than for him to humiliate you before his nobles."

A story about a new social media manager illustrates these points well. Despite her potential and good intentions, her premature attempts at managing a team caused some issues within the group. It would have been wiser for her to wait and let the natural process unfold.

Mistake #20: Insecurity in Leadership

My husband is six foot four, and has the most relaxed, easy-to-get-along-with personality I've ever encountered. (That's just one of the many reasons I married him.) He's fond of joking that some individuals who fall into passive aggression as a defense mechanism have "Napoleon Complex". "Napoleon Complex" is often attributed to those who are shorter in stature, but my husband uses it to describe anyone who feels they must overcompensate for their insecurities by being overly assertive or aggressive. He points out that you don't have to be short to feel small.

This brings us to another ineffective leadership quality I've encountered - the insecure leader. These individuals may possess the title and authority, but they lack the confidence in their own capabilities, which often causes them to react defensively rather than lead proactively. This type of leadership can be detrimental, not only to the leader's personal growth but also to the morale of his team.

An insecure leader might react harshly to constructive criticism, view collaborative suggestions as personal attacks, or micromanage team members in an attempt to maintain control. This behavior stifles creativity and innovation within the team and creates an atmosphere of mistrust and apprehension.

Even worse, he might resort to passive aggressive tactics to get his point across. In one instance, I remember a project leader who would use sarcasm during team meetings as a way to express displeasure or disagreement. It was subtle, but frequent enough that it began to erode the trust and open communication that are so vital for a team's success. Team members started to hold back their ideas, fearing the snide remarks or the eye-rolling responses they might provoke.

It's crucial for leaders to recognize any passive aggressive tendencies they may have and seek help if necessary. Leadership coaching, counseling, or even peer mentorship can provide insecure leaders with the tools they need to build their confidence and learn how to support their team positively.

Mistake #21: Bringing Politics to Work

I get it that you love your country. Really, I do. I love my country too. But the workplace is not the appropriate forum in which to impose political beliefs of any kind upon others. Nor is it a space in which to give others the cold shoulder because they remind you of someone who was recently featured negatively on your news network of choice.

Here's the thing. Not all Millennials are lazy. Not all Boomers are greedy. And believe it or not, most of Generation Z does not actually rely on artificial intelligence to think for them. As leaders, it's time to stop bringing our stereotypes of others to the office. This requires a shift in perspective. A politically-minded leader must learn to separate personal convictions on neutral topics from his professional responsibilities, maintaining a professional environment that fosters respect among all team members. When politics enters the workplace, it often brings with it division and distraction, which can severely impact team performance and cohesion.

In one instance, a manager in our company tried to mediate a heated discussion that had broken out over a new policy proposal that inadvertently touched on political sensitivities. Recognizing the tension, he immediately steered the conversation back to the core issue: how the proposed policy would affect our workflow and client relations, rather than the political implications it might suggest. This approach helped defuse the situation and refocused the team on what truly mattered - our collective objectives.

Leadership in such scenarios is about promoting understanding and teamwork over personal biases. It's about being a mediator who can navigate through sensitive topics without allowing them to derail the team's mission.

Mistake #22: Being Rude as a Leader

The concept of "rudeness" is a fascinating one, as it is perceived differently by each individual. For those from the south, New Yorkers are considered rude due to their often loud and boisterous conversations. On the other hand, northern residents may view midwesterners as rude because it takes time to establish meaningful connections with them. In the workplace, some colleagues may see it as rude for others to interrupt them at their desks for a quick chat about personal matters, while others believe it's impolite not to engage in friendly small talk throughout the day. This ever-evolving idea of what constitutes rudeness makes it a difficult target to pin down and understand. It seems to constantly shift and adapt based on personal experiences and cultural norms.

However, in a leadership role, understanding and adapting to these nuanced perceptions of rudeness is crucial. A leader must be culturally aware and sensitive to the diverse backgrounds and expectations of their team members. This awareness helps in creating an inclusive environment where everyone feels respected and valued.

For instance, a leader might find herself in a multicultural team where the norms for expressing disagreement vary widely. In some cultures, direct confrontation and open disagreement are valued as signs of honesty and engagement; in others, such behaviors might be seen as disrespectful or aggressive. A good leader recognizes these differences and adjusts her communication style to foster a respectful dialogue, ensuring that no member of the team feels alienated or disrespected.

No matter one's cultural origins, certain actions are universally seen as rude. To avoid any potential faux pas, it's best to simply refrain from doing them. The following are a few behaviors that any creative leader should steer clear of at all times.

Interruptions. Firstly, never interrupt another person while she is speaking. Not only is it disrespectful, but it also suggests that you value your own words over theirs. In the realm of leadership, giving every member the chance to express their thoughts fully is essential for fostering an environment of mutual respect and collaboration.

Derogatory Comments or Jokes. Avoid making derogatory comments or jokes at the expense of others. What might seem like harmless fun to some can be deeply offensive or hurtful to others. A leader must set a tone of professionalism and kindness, ensuring that humor does not cross the line into insensitivity.

Failing to Acknowledge Hard Work. Thirdly, do not ignore the contributions of your team members. Failing to acknowledge the hard work and success of your colleagues can lead to feelings of under-appreciation and demotivation. A simple expression of thanks or recognition can go a long way in boosting morale and reinforcing a culture of acknowledgement and reward.

Not Respecting Time. It is important for leaders to maintain punctuality. Being consistently late to meetings or appointments shows a lack of respect for others' time, and suggests poor planning and management skills. Leaders should model the behavior they expect from their team members, and punctuality is a basic but vital aspect of professional conduct.

Demeaning Language or Tone. Using demeaning language or tone can quickly erode respect and trust. Even in moments of frustration or disagreement, it's important for leaders to maintain a level of professionalism that upholds everyone's dignity. Resorting to sarcasm or belittling comments not only hurts individuals but also infects the entire team morale.

Public Criticism. Avoiding public criticism is another key behavior for leaders. Providing feedback is a necessary aspect of leadership, but doing so in a manner that embarrasses someone in front of his peers can lead to resentment and a fear-based work environment. Constructive feedback should be given privately and tactfully, focusing on growth and improvement rather than fault-finding.

By steering clear of these behaviors, leaders can avoid the common pitfall of rudeness in the workplace. Instead, they can cultivate a culture of trust and respect within their teams.

Mistake #23: Being a Doormat

In their efforts to avoid Mistake #22, some leaders inevitably stumble into the trap of Mistake #23. With a desperate determination to maintain peace at all costs, they become Doormat Leaders, passively allowing others to walk all over them and erode their authority. Instead of taking charge and making difficult decisions, they cower in the shadows, afraid of confrontation and conflict. As a result, their teams lack direction and their team members wish that someone would finally stand up for them.

This is where assertiveness comes into play — a crucial skill that every leader must hone. Being assertive doesn't mean being aggressive; it's about being clear and firm with your needs while respecting the needs of others. It's about setting boundaries and enforcing them, communicating expectations clearly, and holding people accountable in a fair and consistent manner.

To escape the pitfalls of becoming a Doormat Leader, one must first recognize the importance of her role as a guide and protector of the team's vision. This involves being proactive rather than reactive, making decisions that align with the team's goals, and not just those that appease the loudest voices. Assertiveness allows leaders to effectively manage resources, direct operations towards productivity, and address issues before they escalate into larger problems.

For instance, consider a scenario where there is a disagreement on team priorities. A Doormat Leader might avoid making any decision that could potentially upset some members. In contrast, an assertive leader would listen to all viewpoints, assess what is best for achieving the team's objectives, and decisively set the course of action, all while explaining her reasoning to ensure everyone understands the rationale behind her decision.

Mistake #24: Checking Ethics at the Door

The worst leader archetype I can think of is the Unethical Leader. This is the person who is willing to overlook hazards and liabilities for the sake of keeping OSHA records clean. He's willing to sweep cash under the table so that his boss can cheat on taxes. He's willing to fire an innocent person in order to satisfy a wrathful client.

These behaviors are far more common than you might think... and it has to stop. This kind of leadership not only destroys the moral fabric of the organization but also undermines the trust and integrity that are crucial for sustained success. Unethical Leaders might achieve short-term gains, but these are often at the expense of long-term stability and reputation.

When leaders choose to "check ethics at the door," they risk creating a culture where employees feel compelled to cut corners, engage in dishonest practices, or worse, participate in illegal activities. This slippery slope can lead to significant legal and financial repercussions for the company, not to mention irreparable damage to its public image.

To combat this, leaders must embrace and embody ethical decision-making as a foundational principle. This involves going beyond merely complying with laws and regulations. Ethical leaders consistently demonstrate fairness, honesty, and respect in every action they undertake and decision they make. They ensure that their actions align with both the letter and the spirit of integrity.

Being an ethical leader means being transparent. This involves being honest about decisions and how they affect both the company and its stakeholders. I have a simple way to test whether or not a decision is ethical: if I wouldn't want it to be publicized on the front page of the New York Times, then perhaps it's not the right decision to make.

Mistake #25: Forgetting That There Are More Than 25 Possible Opportunities to "Get Better" as a Leader

As you flip through the pages of this book, you'll find a treasure trove of 25 opportunities to "Get Better" as a leader in a creative team environment. These invaluable insights barely scratch the surface of all the possible mistakes one can make while leading a team. Drawing from my own experiences, I have shared some of the most common blunders that may arise, though there may be others unique to your situation. My best advice? Stay alert and discerning. Keep your antenna raised for potential trouble, and be prepared to pivot at any moment to avoid allowing harm to enter your creative team environment. True leadership isn't about being perfect or getting everything right; it's about putting your team's well-being first and doing what is right for them.

Summary

In conclusion, leadership within a creative team environment is as challenging as it is rewarding. The myriad pitfalls, from becoming a Doormat Leader to checking ethics at the door, illustrate the complexity and responsibility required to effectively guide a team. Each mistake discussed serves as a lesson in maintaining balance, integrity, and proactive decision-making.

Effective leadership requires a continuous commitment to personal growth and ethical conduct. It demands an openness to feedback, a dedication to acknowledging and rectifying mistakes, and an unyielding pursuit of fostering a respectful and inclusive team culture. By steering clear of the common mistakes outlined in this book and continuously striving to improve, leaders can cultivate an atmosphere that not only drives project success but also contributes to the overall development and satisfaction of every team member.

Remember, the art of leadership is not about authority or power but about empowering others to realize their full potential. It's about making tough choices while maintaining compassion and respect for those you lead. As you move forward with the insights gained from these pages, embrace each challenge as an opportunity to reinforce your commitment to ethical leadership and enhance your effectiveness as a leader in any creative endeavor you undertake.

Chapter 7: Managing Conflict and Criticism

Now, I would like to shift the focus of our study away from what we've learned from past experiences and towards challenges that all leaders of creative teams will inevitably encounter on their leadership journey. Life is full of obstacles and hardships that we all must confront. However, when these challenges arise, we are often caught off guard, wondering "Why me?". It doesn't have to be like this. By taking the time to prepare and plan ahead, we can develop the skills and mindsets needed to face the common challenges that come with being a leader.

Decision making is like a flow chart. Each choice leads to a variety of potential outcomes, which then branch off into even more possibilities. As a leader, I believe it's wise to plan ahead for all of these possible "third generation" outcomes that may come from any decision. This way, when a crisis or challenge arises, we'll be ready with a game plan already in hand.

...But no matter how prepared we think we are, there will always be unexpected challenges that catch us off guard. If you're reading this book, chances are you are a leader of a team that thrives on creativity - so let's discuss five common obstacles that we will all likely encounter at some point in our leadership journeys. The first and perhaps most daunting challenge is managing conflict and criticism.

Managing Conflict and Criticism

As leaders, we have a dual responsibility. We must prepare our teams to handle the inevitable conflicts and criticism that come with being team members. But we also need to equip ourselves to deal with the conflicts and criticism directed at us. Both tasks are challenging. We will quickly discover that each member of our team operates with his own set of values and priorities, as well as varying levels of self-awareness and conflict management skills.

Conflict is a natural part of any team, especially when working with creative individuals. Creative teamwork brings together different ideas, perspectives, and egos. In this chapter, we will explore techniques for effectively managing conflict and criticism within creative teams.

Memories of a particularly challenging incident flood back to me from my time at a small video production company. The pressure was on as we worked tirelessly on a major project for our biggest client yet. Though not a large client, our team of fresh college graduates felt like we had hit the big-time. We entrusted one of our own to direct the project - a moody artist type who wanted to create a masterpiece. While he was talented, it didn't take long for conflicts to arise. Our company owner witnessed a safety protocol being disregarded in pursuit of the perfect shot. And on another occasion, our cast and crew were forced to work three hours past their promised quitting time to finish filming a particular scene. As representatives of our company's name and brand, we knew we needed to address the issue and get our young director to comply with established protocols for safety and man-hours. However, in those days I was still young and foolish - some might say I still am, but I'd like to believe I've grown since then. Instead of approaching the director calmly with potential solutions for moving forward, I stormed in with my own lid flipped and temper flaring. "What in the heck was that?" I demanded.

...I'd started a conflict. And with a moody artist, no less. I should have known better. That particular production turned out to be one of the worst projects I've ever worked on. I've never seen a creative team with such low morale - neither before nor since. Tempers flared, and productivity plummeted.

As a leader, it was a wake-up call for me. I came to the realization that while addressing crucial issues like safety was necessary, my way of handling them needed to shift. The saying "You can catch more flies with honey than with vinegar" comes to mind. If I had been more astute, I could have avoided any conflicts and simply adjusted the project's course. This would have allowed everyone's sense of security and professional fulfillment to remain intact, and morale could have flourished.

The following are a few tips for overcoming the challenge of conflict within your own creative team settings:

Address Conflict Head-On

Handling conflicts with directness and honesty is crucial. Sweeping problems under the rug may seem like an easy solution, but it only makes matters worse. Many leaders make the mistake of ignoring or trying to suppress conflicts, hoping they'll go away on their own. This approach may provide temporary relief, but it can lead to disaster in the future. Unresolved conflicts can brew and create a toxic work environment.

Have you ever been so angry at someone that it consumes your thoughts? The more you think about what to say to him or her, the angrier you become? But when you actually confront the person, the problem is quickly resolved and you feel guilty for having such negative emotions towards them? Don't deny it. We have all experienced this before.

Often, we tend to imagine people as worse than they really are. Our minds can create false scenarios, and our emotions can deceive us. As leaders, we must take control of our feelings instead of letting them control us. We should not avoid conflict, even if it is uncomfortable at first. It is better to endure temporary social discomfort than to let anger simmer and harm our team members from within.

When conflicts arise, leaders must take a proactive approach to addressing them. They should initiate open and honest conversations with all parties involved, clearly expressing their concerns and outlining the specific issues at hand. This level of transparency not only brings clarity to the situation, but also sets a standard for handling conflicts in a professional manner. By openly articulating their concerns, leaders show that they are taking the issue seriously and are committed to finding a resolution. Equally important is the practice of actively listening to others' perspectives. This shows mutual respect and helps build understanding among team members. When leaders genuinely listen to different viewpoints from those involved in a conflict, it creates a collaborative environment where solutions can be co-created. Ultimately, this direct and transparent approach strengthens organizational cohesion by preventing resentment and misunderstandings from building up, promoting a culture of open communication, and enhancing problem-solving abilities. Leaders who embrace this approach not only resolve conflicts effectively, but also role model behaviors that contribute to a healthier and more communicative workplace.

As mentioned in the previous chapter, it is crucial for leaders to avoid passive aggression at all times. Confronting conflicts head-on is a necessary step in breaking free from a passive aggressive mindset. After all, if an issue is directly addressed, there is no need for snide comments or deceitful strategies. A direct confrontation doesn't allow space for such behavior. Therefore, it is important to have difficult conversations, but always with respect and consideration.

Get Used to Criticism

Criticism can come in two forms: constructive or destructive. We must become accustomed to receiving both types. The outside world can be harsh and not everyone will have the same level of social awareness or empathy as you do. It's inevitable that you will receive destructive criticism at some point.

But let's start with something more positive. Constructive criticism is a true gift when delivered by an individual who really cares about your growth. Constructive criticism is aimed at helping you improve. It's specific, actionable, and delivered with empathy. This type of feedback often includes suggestions for how to improve and is framed in a way that acknowledges your efforts and potential.

Picture yourself as a budding author, diligently working on your first novel. You eagerly share a draft with a mentor who offers valuable criticism. She might say, "Your character development is intriguing, but in Chapter 3, you could strengthen the story by showing more of Jane's internal conflict through her actions rather than her thoughts. This would create a stronger connection with the reader." In this scenario, the feedback is focused on enhancing your work, offers a specific suggestion for improvement, and acknowledges the strengths of your draft. This type of critique serves to help you grow by highlighting areas for improvement in a supportive manner.

Constructive feedback is intended to help and guide, while destructive criticism is meant to tear down and discourage. Destructive criticism can be harsh, vague, and lacking empathy. It is not meant to aid in personal growth. In the case of our writer, imagine a scenario where a different reader says, "This book is terrible. You clearly have no clue what you're doing." This type of feedback is destructive because it does not offer any specific suggestions for improvement and is intended to bring the writer down instead of offering assistance.

In the small town of Wilmington, North Carolina, a young Michael Jordan, known for his lightning speed and remarkable agility, was famously cut from his high school basketball team. The cold words of rejection could have crushed his dreams of becoming a professional athlete. But instead, they lit a fire within him. With unwavering determination, he spent countless hours practicing and perfecting his skills on the court. Through sweat and effort, he transformed himself into a powerhouse player - one that would go down in history as one of the greatest basketball players of all time. Despite facing both constructive and destructive criticism throughout his career, Michael Jordan knew how to handle it with grace and tenacity. He could have easily hung up his sneakers and pursued a different career path after being cut from his high school team. But instead, with unshakeable tenacity, he continued to push forward and ultimately achieved unparalleled success in professional basketball. Without his enduring resilience in the face of adversity, the world would have been robbed of witnessing the greatness of Michael Jordan. His ability to rise above criticism is just one of many reasons why he will always be remembered as a legend on and off the court.

As creatives, it is important that we not only brace ourselves for criticism but also actively seek it out. We should be eager to share our work with as many people as possible and ask for honest opinions. Leaders of creative teams can instill the value of constructive criticism by creating an environment where feedback is not only welcome, but expected. Even if a team member is inexperienced in receiving critiques, promoting a culture of open communication within the team will help him learn to appreciate and benefit from feedback.

With that said, leaders must establish a strict rule against destructive criticism among team members. Most teams will face plenty of that from external sources; there's no need to add to it from within. Such criticism only erodes trust and hinders productivity.

As previously mentioned in this section, the world can be a tough place. Not everyone will offer criticism with the intention of helping you improve. Understanding this reality and preparing yourself to handle both constructive and destructive feedback will make you more adaptable and capable in many areas of life, from your career to your personal relationships. Both forms of criticism serve a purpose in personal development. Constructive criticism provides guidance and motivation, while destructive criticism tests your strength and perseverance. By learning how to receive and respond to both types of feedback effectively, you can navigate challenges with greater skill and professionalism.

Set an Expectation of Empathy and Respect

Where are the parents in the house? If you have multiple children, then you surely understand what I mean when I say that letting them bicker is like watching a snowball roll down Mount Everest. It may not seem like a big deal at first, but as it gets bigger and picks up speed, it will eventually become a destructive avalanche that needs to be dealt with.

Sarah had recently taken on the leadership role at a mid-sized design company. The team had been given the critical task of creating a new logo for the upcoming brand launch, with a strict deadline looming. As the pressure continued to mount, Sarah noticed a growing tension amongst team members and a decrease in productivity. Realizing that this was not sustainable, she called for a team meeting to address the issues head-on. During the meeting, it became clear that interpersonal conflicts and unclear communication were contributing to the rising stress levels.

One member of her team, Tom, seemed particularly affected by these issues. Despite his long hours and hard work, he felt undervalued. His frustration was affecting the entire team's dynamic.

Sarah understood the importance of fostering an environment of empathy and respect. She began by acknowledging and appreciating everyone's hard work before inviting them to openly discuss their concerns and challenges. In doing so, Tom expressed feeling overwhelmed and unsupported. He had been hesitant to speak up due to fear of judgment or dismissal.

Sarah listened attentively and reassured him that his contributions were valued, and his concerns were important. She also encouraged other team members to share their perspectives and actively listen to one another. This open dialogue led to several key changes being implemented - from adjusting their workflow and having regular check-ins to ensuring that everyone felt supported and heard. Additionally, Sarah made a conscious effort to recognize individual and team achievements more frequently, creating a culture of appreciation within the team.

The transformation was remarkable. The team's morale improved significantly, and productivity surged as members felt more connected and motivated. The project, which initially seemed on the brink of failure, was completed ahead of schedule and exceeded expectations. Tom, who had been on the verge of burnout, found renewed enthusiasm and a sense of belonging within the team.

Sarah's approach demonstrates why empathy and respect are not just nice-to-haves but essential leadership qualities. Here are a few key takeaways:

Empathy Builds Trust. Sarah's active listening and understanding of her team members' emotions helped build trust and showed that they were valued. This trust is vital for creating a harmonious and cooperative workplace.

Respect Enhances Engagement. When creative team members feel respected and their contributions are acknowledged, they are more engaged and motivated to give their best effort.

Open Communication Prevents Issues. Encouraging open communication helps address issues before they escalate. It fosters a culture where creative team members are comfortable sharing their concerns and collaborating on solutions.

Recognition and Support Drive Performance. Recognizing achievements and providing support when needed boosts morale and can turn challenging situations into opportunities for growth.

Creating a culture of empathy and respect within your team is crucial for cultivating a positive and efficient work environment. It encourages constructive problem-solving, improves team spirit, and ultimately leads to higher performance and results. Leaders who prioritize these principles not only promote a more cohesive workplace but also motivate their teams towards achieving greater success.

Summary

Let's review. To build a healthy creative team that manages conflict and criticism well, remember to:

1. Address Conflict Directly. Deal with issues head-on rather than ignoring them. Honest communication prevents conflicts from festering and helps maintain a healthy work environment.

2. Handle Criticism Wisely. Differentiate between constructive and destructive criticism. Constructive criticism helps you improve and grow, while destructive criticism undermines confidence. Encourage constructive feedback and set boundaries against destructive comments.

3. Foster Empathy and Respect. Cultivate an environment of empathy and respect within the team. Open communication, recognition, and support boost morale and productivity, leading to better team performance and a more positive work atmosphere.

Overall, leaders should approach conflicts and criticism with a balanced, empathetic attitude to build a motivated and effective team.

Chapter 8: Motivating Creative Teams

Tending to a creative team is like tending to a delicate garden – it requires the right mix of nurturing, challenging, and protecting. While creativity may be innate, it needs the right conditions to blossom and bloom. In this chapter, we'll explore essential strategies for fostering a motivating environment for your team, as well as delve into the psychology of creativity and the power of challenges.

To start with, it's important to recognize that creativity is a fragile and sensitive process. It requires a supportive and safe environment in order to thrive. This means creating a workplace culture that encourages risk-taking, experimentation, and open communication. It also means acknowledging and valuing the unique strengths and perspectives of each team member.

Another crucial aspect in fostering creativity is providing challenges. Just as a muscle needs to be strained in order for it to grow, creativity needs challenges and obstacles to thrive. These challenges can come in the form of new projects, deadlines, or even self-imposed goals. They push your team out of their comfort zones and ignite their problem-solving skills, leading to new and innovative ideas. However, it's important to strike a balance between providing challenges and creating burnout. As a leader, it's your responsibility to monitor your team's workload and make sure they have the necessary support and resources to meet their deadlines. Burnout can quickly kill creativity, so it's crucial to address any signs of exhaustion or stress in your team members right away.

Let's look into these topics in greater depth, and discuss some methods for motivating your creative team to achieve greatness.

Understanding the Psychology of Creativity

Before we dive into motivation strategies, it's crucial to understand the unique characteristics of the creative mind. Creative individuals are often driven by intrinsic motivation, seeking personal fulfillment and the satisfaction of creating something new. They are also typically curious and open-minded, constantly seeking new experiences and ideas to fuel their creativity.

However, this comes with its own set of challenges. The creative process can be unpredictable, with highs and lows that can be both exhilarating and exhausting. Creatives may also struggle with self-doubt and perfectionism, which can hinder their productivity and motivation. As a leader, it's important to understand these nuances in order to effectively support your team.

Autonomy

One key factor in promoting creativity is providing autonomy. In my opinion, this is one of the most important principles for any creative leader to grasp. Autonomy means having the freedom to make decisions and take ownership of one's work. Most creative individuals thrive when they have control over their work and are given the freedom to explore new ideas without constant oversight. Micromanaging can stifle creativity and lead to resentment within the team. In order to foster autonomy within your team, you need to create the right conditions. This includes setting clear expectations and boundaries, and empowering team members with the resources they need to succeed. Here are some methods for promoting autonomy in your team:

Clearly Define Goals and Expectations. In order for your team members to have a sense of autonomy, they need to know what is expected of them. Set clear goals and objectives, and communicate them effectively to each team member. This will give them a sense of purpose and direction, while still allowing them the freedom to approach tasks in their own unique ways.

Empower Decision-Making. Give your team members the freedom to make decisions about their work. This can include giving them ownership over certain projects or allowing them to choose their own methods for completing tasks. By trusting your team members to make decisions, you are showing that you value their expertise and ideas.

Provide Resources. In order for your team members to feel autonomous, they may need access to the certain resources and tools. This can include technology, training opportunities, or even flexible work arrangements. Make sure your team members have everything they need in order to successfully carry out their tasks.

Encourage Risk-Taking. Creativity often requires taking risks and trying new things. As a leader, it's important to create a safe space for your team members to take risks without fear of failure or consequence. Encourage experimentation and celebrate failures as learning opportunities.

Remove Micromanagement. Micromanaging is detrimental not only for creativity but also for overall motivation in the workplace. Trust your team members to do their jobs without constant oversight or nitpicking every detail of their work.

Overall, promoting autonomy requires trust and open communication between leaders and their teams. By setting clear goals, providing resources, empowering decision-making, encouraging risk-taking, and removing micromanagement practices, you can create an environment that fosters autonomy and ultimately promotes creativity within your team.

Creative Zig-Zag

It's also essential to recognize that creativity is not a linear process – it involves a lot of trial-and-error and may require multiple iterations before reaching a final product. This means allowing for mistakes and failures along the way without punishing or discouraging them.

Innovation is the process of developing and implementing new ideas that create value. It's about finding new ways to solve problems and improve processes. In today's rapidly changing business landscape, innovation has become a crucial factor for success. Companies that are able to consistently innovate are the ones that stay ahead of the competition. But innovation doesn't just happen by chance – it requires a culture that fosters and supports creativity and risk-taking. As a leader, it's your responsibility to create an environment where innovation can thrive.

Creatives Need Structure (Just Not too Much of It)

Lastly, understanding that creativity requires both structure and flexibility is crucial. While too much structure can stifle creativity, having too little can result in chaos and lack of direction. As a leader, it's your responsibility to strike a balance between providing guidance and giving your team room for experimentation.

The Power of Challenges

As mentioned earlier, challenges are essential in igniting creativity within your team. Challenges force individuals out of their comfort zones, push them to think outside the box, and come up with innovative solutions. As a leader, it's important to create an environment where challenges are not only accepted but encouraged. Here are a few ways you can encourage challenges within your team.

Set Stretch Goals. Instead of setting easily achievable goals, set stretch goals that require your team members to push themselves beyond their limits. This will not only challenge them but also foster a sense of accomplishment when they reach or exceed the goal.

Provide Resources and Support. Make sure your team has access to the necessary resources and support to take on new challenges. This can include training opportunities, access to experts or mentors, or even providing time and space for experimentation.

Lead by Example. As a leader, it's important to lead by example and take on challenges yourself. This will show your team that you are willing to take risks and try new things, which can inspire them to do the same.

Acknowledge Efforts. When your team is taking on challenges, make sure to acknowledge their efforts regardless of the outcome. This will show that you value their hard work and encourage them to continue pushing themselves.

Fail Forward. In order for people to be comfortable taking risks and facing challenges, they need to know that failure is not punished or frowned upon. Instead, frame failures as learning opportunities and use them as a chance for growth and improvement.

By encouraging challenges within your team, you are creating an environment that promotes continuous learning and growth. It also shows that you trust your team members' abilities and believe in their potential for success.

Addressing Burnout and Maintaining Motivation

Burnout is a state of emotional, mental, and physical exhaustion caused by prolonged stress or overwork. It can result in a lack of motivation, decreased productivity, and a negative attitude towards work. As a leader, it's important to be aware of the signs of burnout and take proactive steps to prevent it within your team. First, let's discuss a few telltale signs of burnout that all leaders should be on the lookout for:

Decreased performance and productivity. When once enthusiastic and efficient employees start missing deadlines or producing subpar work, it could be a sign of burnout.

Increased cynicism or negative attitudes. If team members become more cynical or negative about their work or the workplace, this shift in attitude can signal deeper issues.

Physical symptoms. Chronic stress can manifest physically, leading to symptoms like headaches, muscle pain, or a weakened immune system.

Emotional exhaustion. Feelings of being overwhelmed or emotionally drained by work are clear indicators of burnout.

Detachment from work. A noticeable loss of engagement or passion for the job that was once there can be a red flag.

The good news is, burnout can be prevented. Below are some strategies to help manage and prevent burnout among your team.

Encourage Personal Creativity

The creativity of artists and other creative individuals does not disappear when they leave work for the day. In fact, many creatives have ambitious creative pursuits outside of their jobs. Supporting and promoting this personal pursuit of creativity can greatly enhance their performance in the workplace. Encouraging personal creativity among your team members not only helps in keeping their minds sharp and innovative but also allows them an outlet to express themselves in ways that are most fulfilling to them.

I have a friend who leads a double life: by day, he works as a video editor for a national network, but by night, he pursues his passion as an independent film director. His supervisor encourages his personal creative pursuits and allows him to take extended unpaid leave once or twice a year to focus on his own projects. And when he returns, his job is always waiting for him. While this may seem like an extraordinary arrangement - and admittedly not every employer can afford it - my friend's loyalty to his job is unwavering. He is grateful for the support and flexibility his company has shown him, and would go above and beyond for them in return.

As a leader, fostering an environment where personal projects are recognized and valued can lead to increased job satisfaction and overall happiness within the team. Here's how you can support personal creativity:

Provide Flexibility in Schedules. Allowing flexible work hours or remote working days gives team members the time they may need to engage in creative activities outside of work. This flexibility shows that you respect and value their needs for a work-life balance.

Celebrate Creative Endeavors. Make it a point to show interest in the personal creative projects of your team members. Whether it's through a casual conversation or highlighting these endeavors at team meetings, acknowledging their creative pursuits can boost morale and inspire others.

Create a Sharing Environment. Encourage the sharing of creative interests during team interactions. This can be facilitated through regular 'project sharing' sessions where team members present their side projects. This not only strengthens team bonds but also fosters a culture of creativity and inspiration.

Offer Resources and Tools. If possible, provide resources that could assist in their personal creative projects. This could range from software tools, books, online courses, or even just space like meeting rooms.

Prioritize Self-Care

Prioritizing self-care in the workplace is crucial for maintaining a healthy and happy team. The demands of work can often lead to stress and burnout, but by encouraging self-care activities, leaders can help their team members find balance and improve their overall well-being. Here are some tips for incorporating self-care into the workplace culture:

Encourage Physical Activity. Exercise has been shown to not only improve physical health but also mental health. Encourage your team members to take breaks throughout the day to stretch or go for a walk. You could even organize fitness challenges or group workouts.

Lead by Example. As a leader, it's important to practice self-care yourself. Make sure you're taking breaks when needed, prioritizing your own mental and physical health, and setting boundaries between work and personal life.

Allow Time Off. It's important for team members to have time off from work to recharge and focus on their own needs. Encourage them to use their vacation days or offer occasional mental health days.

Support Hobbies. Hobbies are a great way for individuals to relax and recharge outside of work. Encourage your team members to pursue hobbies they enjoy by offering flexible schedules or resources that may be helpful.

Note: It must be emphasized that for those working in a creative field, being an artist is not a hobby; it is a profession. A filmmaker does not come home from her job on set and continue to make more films for leisure. For a filmmaker, a leisure activity might be something like cooking or gardening. But any form of filmmaking - whether on the clock or in her free time - is a way to advance her career. The same applies to graphic designers and other types of creatives as well. Any type of work they do in their field should be seen as a professional move, and not just a pastime.

Intrinsic Motivation

Creative individuals are often driven by intrinsic motivation, seeking personal fulfillment rather than external rewards. This can make them less inspired by extrinsic motivators, such as bonuses or promotions. Don't get me wrong. Everyone loves a promotion. But some creatives find other things even more motivating than career power. For instance, here are a few intrinsic values that many creatives find rewarding:

Autonomy. Many creatives relish the feeling of being in complete control of their work, able to mold and shape it as they please. The freedom to delve into ideas without any outside limitations is a precious gift, one that fuels their creativity and drives them forward. With no restraints holding them back, they can fully explore the depths of their imaginations: and push the boundaries of what is possible. Providing a sense of autonomy and self-direction at work may become a motivator that is cherished above all else, providing a sense of fulfillment and satisfaction that cannot be found elsewhere.

Mastery. Most creatives have an internal relentless determination that drives them towards personal growth and the constant honing of their skills and abilities. With every step forward, they push themselves to reach new heights and become the best versions of themselves. These individuals are highly motivated by opportunities to truly master their chosen career fields.

Purpose. For certain artists, their passion and drive comes from a strong sense of purpose and mission. Each stroke of the brush, every word written, and every musical note played is carefully selected to convey a unique message to the world. When an artist works with such intention and purpose, she is often inspired by opportunities to take part in creative projects that have a deeper meaning or make a positive impact on society.

Summary

In conclusion, managing a team—especially a creative one—requires sensitivity to the individual needs of its members and a proactive approach to fostering an environment that supports these needs. Through flexibility, support for personal pursuits, prioritization of self-care, and a deep appreciation for intrinsic motivation, leaders can cultivate a workplace that truly values its most important asset: its people. This will not only prevent burnout but also unlock the full creative potential of the team, driving innovation and success in today's competitive landscape.

Chapter 9: Building a Positive Work Culture

I've heard it said that "culture" is how your heart and your stomach feels on a Sunday night about the upcoming work week. In the ever-evolving world of creative industries, where innovation and self-expression reign supreme, the cultivation of a positive work culture is not just an appealing goal but a crucial ingredient for success. A flourishing environment for creativity empowers individuals to unleash their full potential, nurtures collaboration and ultimately fuels the creation of groundbreaking work. In this chapter, we will dive into essential strategies for constructing such a culture, carefully crafted to meet the specific needs and sensibilities of creative professionals.

First and foremost, building a culture that aligns with the ethos of creative professionals requires an understanding of what drives them. Creativity is not merely a skill but a way of living and seeing the world. Therefore, any work culture aimed at nurturing creativity must prioritize psychological safety and provide a space where creative minds feel both valued and understood.

Embracing the Power of Psychological Safety

At the heart of a positive work culture lies psychological safety – the unwavering belief that one can speak up, question assumptions, and share ideas without fear of repercussions. Creative professionals, often characterized by their penchant for risk-taking and unconventional thinking, thrive in environments where vulnerability is embraced rather than shunned.

This embrace not only enables them to explore unconventional ideas but also empowers them to challenge the status quo and bring innovative solutions to the table without the fear of judgment or failure. An environment rich in psychological safety encourages a continuous flow of open communication and collaborative risk-taking, which are pivotal for creative breakthroughs.

To foster an environment of psychological safety, consider the following tips:

Stop fearing failure. Failure isn't the end of the world. Some leaders view failure as a devastating, possibly career-ending occurrence, which then discourages their team members from taking risks. In reality, failure is nothing but a learning experience.

Encouraging a culture that perceives failure as a stepping stone rather than a stumbling block requires constant reinforcement from leadership. Leaders should openly share their own failures and lessons learned, creating an atmosphere where mistakes are seen as part of the creative process. This openness not only demystifies failure but also humanizes the leaders, making them more relatable and approachable.

Encourage experimentation. Recognize and reward risk-taking, even when it doesn't lead to success. Encouraging experimentation goes hand in hand with normalizing failure. It's about creating a safe space where creative professionals can test out their ideas without the looming fear of negative consequences. This means providing resources and time for experimentation and celebrating the process as much as the product.

Provide adequate resources. There's little more frustrating to any employee than being given a directive, without being provided with the necessary resources to accomplish it. Whether it be software, subscription-based content, or even something as basic as a company laptop, ensuring that creative professionals have what they need is vital.

With the rise of remote work, it has become common for companies to hire employees who are expected to provide their own work laptops and software licenses. I strongly disagree with this practice. When employers expect employees to bring their own resources to complete company work, they are essentially treating the employees as contractors or temporary freelancers. This can cause them to feel expendable, believing that their employment contract could be terminated at any time - (after all, the company has very little invested in their work!). To foster a sense of permanence and stability within your team, it is important to treat your employees like full-time members by providing company-issued laptops and software licenses.

Minimize bureaucracy. Streamline processes and reduce unnecessary red tape to empower individuals to take ownership of their work and make decisions swiftly. Innovation thrives when creativity is not entangled in cumbersome procedures. By minimizing bureaucracy, you allow creative professionals the liberty to quickly execute their ideas and adapt to ever-changing scenarios. This agility is particularly crucial in the creative industry where trends and consumer expectations can shift dramatically and with little warning.

Prioritizing Work-Life Balance

The concept of work-life balance is so crucial that the entire next chapter is dedicated to unpacking its nuances. But work-life balance is a vital element of workplace culture, so we will touch briefly on it here. Creative work, often characterized by its demanding nature and unpredictable deadlines, can take a toll on individuals' well-being. To prevent burnout and maintain a positive work culture, try implementing the following tips:

Flexible Work Arrangements. Offering flexible options such as remote work, flexible hours, or compressed workweeks can go a long way in promoting work-life balance. This allows employees to manage their schedules around their personal commitments while still completing their tasks effectively.

Encourage Breaks and Recharge. Make it a policy to encourage taking regular breaks throughout the day as well as utilizing allotted vacation days. This helps prevent creative burnout and keeps productivity and morale high. Leaders should lead by example, taking their own vacations and openly discussing the benefits of rest and recuperation.

Mindfulness and Wellness Programs. Promote Mental Health Awareness. Encourage open discussions about mental health, provide access to wellness resources, and ensure that managers are trained to recognize signs of stress and burnout. This approach not only supports the well-being of employees but also contributes to a more productive and harmonious workplace.

Recognize and Reward Efforts. A key aspect of creating and maintaining a positive work culture is acknowledging and celebrating the hard work and dedication of employees. This not only boosts morale but also encourages motivation, productivity, and overall job satisfaction.

Fostering a Sense of Purpose and Meaning

Creative professionals are often driven by a desire to make a meaningful impact on the world. To tap into this drive, it's necessary to cultivate a team culture that not only produces excellent work but also maintains a clear and authentic purpose that resonates with its members. This purpose should go beyond mere profit generation; it should connect to broader societal contributions and personal growth opportunities.

A well-defined mission that aligns with the values of creative professionals can inspire them to invest more deeply in their work. When team members understand how their daily efforts contribute to a larger vision, they are more likely to feel valued and engaged. Articulate your team's mission clearly and revisit it regularly to ensure it remains relevant and motivating.

When crafting a mission statement for a creative team, it's important to consider the unique motivations and values that drive creatives. This could include themes such as:

Contributing to society. Many creative professionals are drawn to their work because they want to make a positive impact on the world. Incorporating this desire into your mission statement can inspire employees to invest more deeply in their work.

Personal growth. Creatives are often passionate about continuously developing their skills and pushing themselves outside of their comfort zones. Highlighting opportunities for personal growth and development in your mission statement can appeal to this drive.

Innovation and creativity. Creative industries thrive on innovation and pushing boundaries. Your mission statement should reflect this value and encourage employees to think outside the box.

Collaboration. Creativity often thrives in collaborative environments where diverse perspectives come together. Emphasize the importance of teamwork in your mission statement to foster a culture of collaboration.

Once you have defined your shared mission, it's crucial to consistently reexamine it with your team. Remind them how their work contributes towards achieving this goal, celebrate milestones that align with it, and make sure any new initiatives or projects are in line with the mission. This will help keep everyone aligned and motivated.

Continuous Learning and Development

In the fast-paced world of creative industries, staying ahead of the curve is essential. As a leader, it's your responsibility to create an environment that supports ongoing learning and development within the team. The following are some key strategies for fostering a culture of continuous learning and development:

Encourage Curiosity. Curiosity is the driving force behind creativity, and it's essential for continuous learning. Encourage your team members to ask questions, explore new ideas, and seek out knowledge in areas outside of their job descriptions. This could involve providing opportunities for employees to attend conferences, workshops, or webinars related to their field or other areas of interest.

Promote Cross-Training Opportunities. Cross-training is an effective way to broaden employees' skill sets and foster a more well-rounded team. This involves giving individuals the chance to learn tasks or skills from colleagues in different roles within the organization. Not only does this provide valuable learning opportunities, but it also promotes collaboration and understanding amongst team members.

Invest in Professional Development. Providing your team with access to professional development resources such as courses, certifications, or coaching can have significant benefits for both employees and the organization as a whole. It shows that you are invested in their growth and helps them stay up-to-date with industry trends and best practices.

Create a Mentorship Program. Pairing more experienced team members with those who are newer to the industry can be highly beneficial for both parties involved. Mentors can pass down valuable knowledge and experience while mentees gain insight into career progression opportunities.

Foster a Growth Mindset. Promoting a growth mindset within your team is crucial for fostering a culture of continuous learning and development. A growth mindset is the belief that intelligence and abilities can be developed through dedication and hard work. This contrasts with a fixed mindset, which believes that intelligence and ability are innate traits that cannot be changed. As a leader, it's essential to promote a growth mindset among your team members.

Recognize and Reward Curiosity. Celebrate employees' willingness to explore new ideas and experiment with different approaches. Sometimes, even the smallest efforts can lead to significant breakthroughs or successes. Make sure to acknowledge and appreciate the effort and dedication each team member puts into his work, even if the results may not be immediately visible.

Fairness and Equity

Fairness and equity are essential components of a successful team culture. When opportunities for learning and development are not distributed fairly, it can create feelings of resentment and hinder the growth of individual team members as well as the organization as a whole. To ensure that all team members have access to learning and development opportunities, consider implementing the following strategies:

Identify Individual Development Needs. Each team member has unique skills, interests, and career aspirations. As a leader, it's crucial to understand each employee's individual development needs to provide relevant growth opportunities.

Provide Equal Access. It's important to ensure that all team members have equal access to learning and development resources. This includes considering factors such as location, scheduling constraints, and financial barriers when planning training or professional development opportunities.

Offer Diverse Learning Methods. Different people learn in different ways. Some may prefer traditional classroom-style training, while others may prefer self-paced online courses or one-on-one coaching sessions. Offering diverse learning methods ensures that everyone can engage in professional growth in a way that best suits his or her needs.

Be Transparent and Communicate Clearly. When promoting learning and development opportunities, be transparent about the selection process and criteria for participation. Clear communication will help alleviate any potential misunderstandings or feelings of unfair treatment.

Address Biases. It's essential to address any unconscious biases that may exist within the team. Unconscious biases are deeply ingrained attitudes and stereotypes that affect our decision-making processes and perception of others. These biases can be harmful when it comes to promoting learning and development opportunities within a team.

Respect

Respect is a crucial aspect of building a positive team culture. When team members feel respected by their peers and leaders, it creates a sense of trust, collaboration, and mutual support within the team. In contrast, a lack of respect can lead to conflicts, misunderstandings, and an overall toxic work environment. Here are some ways to promote respect within your team:

Active Listening. One of the key elements of respect is actively listening to others' ideas and perspectives. When team members feel heard and understood, they are more likely to engage in open communication and share their thoughts without fear of judgment or dismissal.

As a leader, it's essential to model active listening by giving your full attention when someone is speaking and asking clarifying questions to ensure you understand his perspective fully. Encourage your team members to do the same to create a culture where everyone's voices are valued.

Open Communication. Respectful communication involves being direct, honest, and transparent while also considering other people's feelings. It's crucial to establish clear communication channels within your team so that everyone feels comfortable sharing his thoughts, concerns, or feedback openly.

Regular Check-Ins. Check-ins are an effective way to show respect for your team members' well-being. These can be informal one-on-one conversations or structured group discussions where individuals can express any challenges she may be facing.

When conducting check-ins, make sure to actively listen without judgment or offering immediate solutions. Sometimes all someone needs is someone else who understands and empathizes with him.

Boundaries. Respecting each other's boundaries is vital in maintaining positive working relationships. Everyone has different personal preferences when it comes to work styles, communication methods, or time management. As a leader, it's important to understand these differences and respect each person's boundaries. For example, some employees may prefer face-to-face interactions while others may prefer emails or messaging platforms. Some may prefer strict work hours while others may need flexibility to accommodate their personal commitments. By respecting these boundaries, you contribute to the team member's sense of psychological safety and feeling of being heard and valued.

Summary

In conclusion, creating a positive and productive team culture requires a multifaceted approach that encompasses continuous learning and development, fairness and equity, and respect among all team members. As leaders, it's our responsibility to ensure that our mission statements not only reflect these values but also actively promote them in everyday practices. By doing so, we foster an environment where innovation thrives, collaboration is encouraged, and every team member feels valued and respected.

Implementing these strategies will help build a strong foundation for your team's success. It will also position your organization as a forward-thinking and dynamic place where talented professionals seek to contribute their skills. Ultimately, the benefits of such an approach extend beyond individual team members, enhancing overall organizational performance and reputation in the creative industry.

Remember, the journey towards creating an optimal team culture is ongoing and requires commitment, reflection, and adaptability. Keep engaging with your team, soliciting their feedback, and making necessary adjustments to ensure that your culture remains vibrant and creative. In doing so, you will not only achieve your organizational goals but also empower each member of your team to reach her full potential.

Chapter 10: Work-Life Balance for Creative Professionals

Within the fast-paced and ever-evolving world of creative professions, achieving a healthy work-life balance can seem like an insurmountable task. The relentless demands to constantly innovate, produce at a high level, and stay on top of the latest trends can quickly become overwhelming. However, it is crucial to keep in mind that maintaining a good work-life balance is not simply about avoiding burnout; it also plays a significant role in nurturing creativity, enhancing overall well-being, and setting the stage for long-term success. The delicate balancing act between work and personal life is like walking along a tightrope, requiring constant focus and attention to ensure stability and harmony. Without this balance, one risks falling into the depths of exhaustion and disillusionment.

In this chapter, we will dive into effective strategies and practical tips for maintaining a harmonious work-life balance among your team of creative professionals. From empowering team members to establish healthy boundaries, to teaching them valuable time management skills, to promoting opportunities for self-care and prioritizing both physical and mental well-being, we will explore the various elements that contribute to a positive and sustainable work-life balance within a creative team setting. By implementing these techniques, you can create an environment where individuals are able to thrive not only in their professional roles, but also in their personal lives.

Understanding the Importance of Work-Life Balance

Your team consists of single moms, busy spouses, people who are caring for elderly parents, dads who coach little league after hours, and a myriad of other individuals whose lives don't end at 5 o'clock. The concept of work-life balance is crucial for creative professionals, as it allows them to maintain a healthy and sustainable lifestyle.

I was once asked during a job interview, "Do you ever plan on having kids? Because you should know that this job requires you to work from nine to five on weekdays, with frequent additional nights and weekends." The insinuation was, "If you choose to accept this job offer, I'm already judging you for being a terrible mom." Not only are questions like this illegal to ask, but the manager telegraphed that my time wouldn't be respected and that it would be impossible for me to maintain any sort of work-life balance within that position. Needless to say, I had a much diminished interest in the role after that interview.

This experience was a poignant reminder of the importance of cultivating an environment that respects and supports the diverse needs of its team members. It underscored the necessity for leadership to not only understand but to actively promote work-life balance as an integral part of the workplace culture. The implications of neglecting this balance are significant, not just for individual team members but for the organization as a whole.

To begin addressing these challenges within your own creative team, start by openly discussing the concept of work-life balance. Encourage dialogue about what this looks like for each person, acknowledging that one size does not fit all. Some may need flexible hours to drop kids at school or care for a family member, while others might require quiet days dedicated to deep work without meetings to foster creativity and productivity.

Moreover, consider implementing structured yet flexible policies that accommodate various life commitments without sacrificing work output. This could involve remote working options, adjustable working hours, or even job-sharing models where feasible. The key is to provide options that help individuals manage their professional and personal responsibilities effectively.

It is vital to lead by example. If management stresses the importance of work-life balance but regularly sends emails late at night, expectations become muddled. Leaders should demonstrate through their actions that they value and practice this balance themselves, which in turn legitimizes it within the team.

Not convinced yet that promoting a positive work-life balance is worth the hype? Here are a few additional perks.

Increased Creativity. When your team members have time to rest and recharge, their minds are given the space to wander and make new connections. This leads to an increased flow of creativity and can result in fresh ideas and innovative solutions.

Improved Mental and Physical Health. Constant stress and burnout can have negative effects on both mental and physical health. By achieving a good work-life balance, individuals can reduce stress levels, improve their moods, and boost their overall well-being (thus boosting their abilities to communicate tactfully and professionally at work).

Better Productivity. When one's workload is balanced and not overwhelming, she is more likely to be productive and efficient. Taking breaks and prioritizing tasks helps individuals stay focused and avoid wasting time on unnecessary activities.

Greater Job Satisfaction. A healthy work-life balance often leads to greater job satisfaction and fulfillment. When individuals feel in control of their time and are able to balance their work with personal life, they are more likely to be happy and engaged in their careers. It ultimately creates a positive working environment for all involved.

What are the most effective ways to create an atmosphere that supports a positive balance between work and personal life? Throughout this chapter, we will examine various tactics for guaranteeing that all team members prioritize a well-rounded approach to their professional lives.

Setting Boundaries

One of the most crucial steps in achieving a healthy work-life balance is establishing boundaries. This means creating clear, defined limits between team members' professional time and personal time. For instance, one approach could be setting a policy where emails sent after a certain hour are not expected to be answered until the next working day. This ensures that team members can truly disconnect after hours, protecting their personal time and mental space from work intrusion. Additionally, managers can lead by example by avoiding scheduling meetings during times that are typically reserved for personal activities, such as early mornings or late evenings.

I would be remiss not to mention... not all boundaries are healthy. It is entirely possible that a creative team member might have an unrealistic idea of what his role in teamwork might look like. This is where regular check-ins and clear communication about roles, responsibilities, and expectations play a crucial role. Understanding that each team member might have different expectations based on his personal circumstances, managers should strive to provide clarity and consistency in their messaging. This helps in preventing misunderstandings and ensuring that boundaries enhance productivity rather than hinder it.

For instance, if a team member prefers uninterrupted mornings to focus on creative tasks, setting a boundary like "no meetings before noon" can be communicated and respected by the rest of the team. However, this must be balanced with team needs, such as coordinating with other members who may have their own preferences or constraints.

Not sure which boundaries are healthy, and which ones are not? The following are some helpful tips for identifying and implementing positive boundaries in a creative team environment:

Define Your Work Hours. Take the time to determine when you will start and end your work day. Make a commitment to sticking to this schedule as much as possible, and try to avoid working overtime or on weekends unless absolutely necessary.

Create a Dedicated Workspace. It can be tempting to work from anywhere, but having a designated area in your home or office solely for work can be highly beneficial. This physical separation can help you mentally switch from "work mode" to "personal mode."

Limit Work-Related Activities Outside of Work Hours. Encourage team members to resist the urge to check emails or take work calls after their designated work hours have ended. By allowing themselves time away from work responsibilities, your team can fully relax and recharge during their personal time.

Note: This can be difficult for creative employees. Creatives tend to do their best work at odd hours, and don't always thrive in a 9-5 capacity. If necessary, look for outside-the-box ways to allow your creative team members access to those "prime brain-power time-frames" (even if it's late at night), while still unplugging from work regularly to recharge.

It is crucial to have open communication about boundaries with your team members, clients, and loved ones. As a leader, it is important to set clear expectations and respect the boundaries of others. Your team members should also feel empowered to communicate their own boundaries. It is common for leaders to view team members who set personal boundaries as insubordinate or not committed enough. However, this kind of thinking can be detrimental. Just because a team member does not openly communicate her boundaries does not mean she does not have any. Everyone has boundaries that should be respected. If you do not allow your team member to communicate her boundaries, she may still enforce them without your knowledge, leading to confusion and interruptions in performance. As a leader, it is always beneficial to encourage open communication and understanding of each other's boundaries within the team. In doing so, you can foster a more productive and harmonious work environment for everyone involved.

Managing Time Effectively

Maintaining a healthy work-life balance requires effective time management skills. By equipping your team with the necessary tools and techniques to manage their time efficiently, you can help them achieve more in less hours, leaving ample space for personal activities, which boost creativity and reduce burnout.

Time management isn't just about keeping a calendar; it involves prioritizing tasks, breaking down projects into manageable pieces, and understanding each team member's peak productive periods. For creatives, whose work often depends on unpredictable bursts of inspiration, traditional time management methods can sometimes fall short. Instead, consider introducing techniques tailored to harness creativity while still respecting the clock.

For instance, implementing the Pomodoro Technique can be particularly effective. This method involves working in focused sprints of 25 minutes followed by a five-minute break. These intervals, known as Pomodoros, help maintain high levels of concentration while preventing fatigue. After four Pomodoros, a longer break of 15-30 minutes is recommended—perfect for a creative recharge.

Another approach is the use of time blocking. Encourage your team members to block out periods in their schedules for specific activities.

This not only allocates time for deep focus on tasks but also provides clear boundaries for switching between professional and personal activities. For example, a designer might block three hours in the morning for conceptual development when his creative energy is highest, leaving administrative tasks for the afternoon when he may feel more structured.

Here are a few additional time management strategies that can be implemented:

Prioritize Tasks. Teach your team how to prioritize their tasks based on urgency and importance. This helps them tackle high-priority projects first and saves less crucial tasks for later. This method not only ensures that critical tasks get the attention they deserve but also helps in reducing the stress of last-minute rushes.

Use Technology Wisely. Encourage the use of technology to streamline tasks. From project management tools like Trello or Asana to time tracking apps like Toggle or RescueTime, these resources help manage workload and stay on track with deadlines. However, caution against over-reliance on technology as it can lead to distractions.

Break Projects into Smaller Tasks. Large projects can be daunting and may seem insurmountable at first glance. By breaking them down into manageable pieces, tasks become less intimidating and easier to handle. This approach not only simplifies the work but also provides a clear roadmap towards completion.

Allow me to indulge in two personal soapbox topics. First, encourage checking emails less frequently and at designated times. I once worked for an executive manager who regularly reminded all of the company staff members that he would respond to all relevant emails within 48 hours, but most likely not within the first 3 hours. This is because he intentionally looked at his emails only 3 times a day - once at about

8:30 in the morning, once for about 15 minutes right after lunch, and once more just before he left for the day. That's it. If we emailed him at 9:00 am, it would have to wait. His notification sounds were turned off. His email app was closed. He was busy doing other work, and would not allow himself to be interrupted by any distractions.

I've since adopted this manager's approach to checking emails. I don't know about you, but when I turn on my email's notification sounds, my laptop starts to sound like a church handbell choir. Every time that "chime" sounds, I rush to the inbox to see if I'd just gotten that important message I'd been waiting for, but alas… it was only another marketing message bound for the trash bin. This approach of checking emails less frequently not only improved my productivity but also significantly reduced the stress associated with constant interruptions. It allowed me to focus more deeply on the tasks at hand, which is crucial in a creative environment where concentration and flow are key to producing quality work.

Secondly, as creatives, we need to learn the difference between "urgent" and "important". This distinction is crucial not only in professional settings but also in personal life. Something urgent requires immediate attention, but it might not necessarily have a long-term impact on your goals. Conversely, important tasks are those that contribute to long-term missions and aspirations but might not need immediate action.

Very often, especially in the business world, immature leaders will try to motivate workers into action by making everything "urgent". When these leaders see the frenzied activity of their staff, they enjoy a few internal moments of satisfaction, because they feel like things are getting done. But remember - it's only a feeling. "Urgency" is usually driven by emotion. "Importance" is driven by consequence. Particularly if you are a middle manager who is leading a creative team, you'll want to be finely attuned to the distinction between "urgency" and "importance". You are your team's shield from immature executive leadership. Don't allow a sense of chronic urgency and frenzied activity to be a baseline in your team's culture.

You might ask, how should we prioritize tasks to determine which is important, which is merely urgent, and which is neither? I'm glad you asked! We'll talk about that in the next section.

Prioritizing Tasks

In addition to managing your time effectively, it is important to prioritize your tasks. This ensures that you are focusing on the right activities at the right time, which can significantly enhance your productivity and reduce feelings of overwhelm. Understanding the Eisenhower Matrix can be a valuable tool here. This method divides tasks into four categories: urgent and important, important but not urgent, urgent but not important, and neither urgent nor important. By categorizing tasks this way, you can clearly see what needs your immediate attention and what can wait, thereby managing your workload more effectively.

For instance, tasks that are both urgent and important need to be dealt with immediately—these are the fires you need to put out. Tasks that are important but not urgent can be scheduled for a bit later; these often involve planning or long-term growth strategies which are crucial but don't have to disrupt your current workflow. Tasks that are urgent but not important should be delegated if possible—these might include some emails or phone calls that need quick answers but don't necessarily require your specific expertise. Finally, tasks that are neither urgent nor important should be dropped or postponed indefinitely. These might include unsolicited offers or non-essential meetings that do not contribute to your core objectives.

To implement this strategy effectively, start each day or week by reviewing your to-do list and categorizing each task according to the Eisenhower Matrix. This will give you a clear roadmap of your priorities and help in managing your time more efficiently. It's also helpful to review this matrix regularly as priorities can shift.

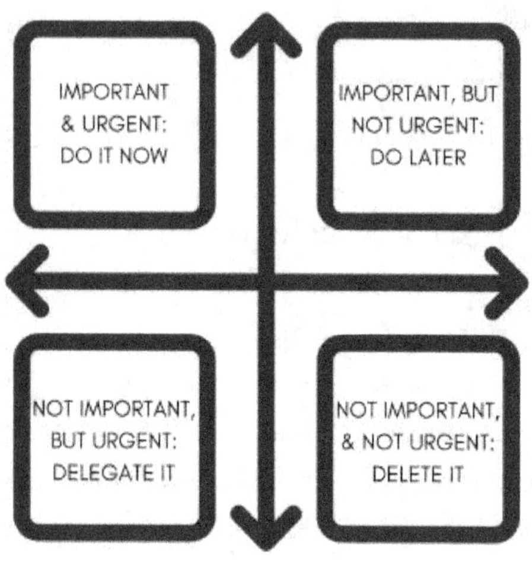

HERE ARE SOME WAYS to effectively match tasks to their correct boxes within an Eisenhower Matrix:

Assess the Impact. Look at each task and determine the impact it has on your goals. Tasks that have a direct and significant impact on achieving key objectives should be given higher priority.

Consider the Effort. Analyze how much effort each task requires. Sometimes, it might be more efficient to complete several smaller, less effort-intensive tasks to clear your schedule for bigger projects.

Set Clear Goals. Having clear, actionable goals for each day can help in prioritizing tasks that align directly with reaching these goals.

Within these guidelines, I offer one final nugget of wisdom: Avoid perfectionism. Perfectionism can be a major productivity killer. Recognizing when good is good enough is essential, especially in a fast-paced work environment. Perfectionism can not only delay the completion of tasks but also lead to burnout and decreased job satisfaction. It's crucial to balance quality with efficiency, knowing when to move forward rather than getting stuck in the minute details.

By teaching your team how to prioritize their work efficiently, you not only enhance their productivity but also help in maintaining a good work-life balance, as they can allocate time more effectively between their professional responsibilities and personal interests.

Taking Care of Your Physical and Mental Health

A good work-life balance is not just about managing your time and setting boundaries; it is also about taking care of your physical and mental health. Regular exercise, adequate sleep, and proper nutrition are fundamental aspects of maintaining overall health, which in turn contributes to more effective work performance and personal satisfaction. Encouraging employees to integrate wellness practices into their daily routines can boost morale and productivity. For instance, implementing "walking meetings" instead of traditional conference-room gatherings can provide physical activity and a change of scenery, sparking more creative ideas and solutions.

Additionally, emphasizing the importance of mental breaks throughout the day is vital. Encouraging short "brain breaks" where employees can step away from their desks helps in resetting their minds, which is crucial for sustained concentration and productivity. Companies increasingly recognize that mental health is as important as physical health; hence, providing resources such as access to counseling services or wellness apps can help in supporting an employee's overall well-being.

Creating a supportive work environment also extends to recognizing the signs of burnout. Educating managers on how to identify and address burnout is key. Simple actions such as acknowledging hard work, adjusting workloads, or allowing flexible working hours can make a significant difference. A culture that prioritizes employee well-being not only enhances productivity but also fosters loyalty and decreases turnover rates.

Furthermore, cultivating a community at work where employees feel valued and part of a team contributes significantly to job satisfaction. Organizing team-building activities that are not necessarily work-related can strengthen relationships among colleagues and create a more cohesive team environment.

To break it down, the following are main points to keep in mind when developing a work culture that promotes the whole-life wellness of team members.

Encourage Physical Activity. Promote the incorporation of regular physical activities into daily routines. This could be as simple as taking short "walking meetings" or organizing team sports events. Physical activity not only boosts physical health but also elevates mood and energy levels, enhancing productivity.

Focus on Nutrition. Advocate for a balanced diet rich in nutrients. Consider offering healthy eating options if you provide meals or snacks at the workplace. Proper nutrition supports cognitive function and energy levels throughout the day.

Stress Management Techniques. Teach stress-reduction methods such as mindfulness, and taking varying forms of "brain breaks". These practices help in managing work-related stress and foster a state of mental well-being.

Ensure Adequate Rest. Encourage employees to get enough sleep each night. Lack of sleep can lead to decreased attention and cognitive function, which can significantly impact job performance and safety.

Mental Health Resources. Provide access to mental health resources and support. This may include employee assistance programs, counseling services, or workshops focused on mental health topics.

Work-life balance is dynamic and adjusting it is an ongoing process. Regularly check in with your team to assess their needs, and to provide options when needed.

Final Tips for Creating a Culture that Encourages Positive Work-Life Balance

When it comes to promoting a healthy work-life balance within creative teams, there's no one-size-fits all solution. Every team is different and each individual is unique. Therefore, as a leader, it's your job to compile these ideas into a plan that works for your team. I leave you with a few final tips that may be helpful when used in conjunction with the above strategies for building a team culture that values work-life balance.

Encourage Team Members to Find a Creative Outlet Outside of Work. Embracing a passion for creativity beyond the workplace can invigorate the mind and prevent burnout. Whether it's painting, writing, playing an instrument, or gardening, having an outlet for self-expression can help your team members stay inspired and refreshed.

Network with Other Creatives. Surround your team with other creatives who can help foster camaraderie and provide fresh perspectives and collaboration opportunities. Attend industry events, join vibrant online communities, or participate in stimulating creative meetups.

Set Realistic Goals. Ambitious goals are important, but it's crucial to set attainable objectives and avoid overwhelming your team members. Break down larger aspirations into smaller, more manageable steps.

Celebrate Your Accomplishments. Don't forget to take time to acknowledge and celebrate your team's achievements, no matter how small they may seem. This will boost morale and keep the team motivated to continue pushing towards goals.

Summary

Creating a harmonious work-life balance is an ever-evolving journey that demands dedication and perseverance. However, the rewards of achieving it are invaluable. By establishing clear boundaries, allowing team members to effectively manage their own schedules, prioritizing tasks, and nurturing both the physical and emotional well-being of team members, you can craft a sustainable and gratifying workplace environment that enables creative team members to flourish in all aspects of life.

Chapter 11: In Conclusion

As we draw to the end of our exploration on the qualities that make a remarkable leader of creative teams, I impart this final thought: Leadership is not a skill that can be obtained solely through formal education or previous managerial roles. It calls for an open mind, a readiness to modify and evolve, and a selfless dedication to prioritize the needs of your team above your own. It is the essence of true leadership - a nurturing spirit that fosters growth and inspires greatness in others.

A Leader's Personal Wants and Needs Take Second Place

In order to be a truly effective leader, one must let go of the pursuit of personal fulfillment and individual success. While these may be desirable goals, they become less important once you take on the role of a leader. The focus shifts from oneself to the team that is being led. It becomes about the growth, development, and success of the team members. A leader who puts the team's interests first will often find that individual team members are more willing to invest their energy and creativity in projects. They feel valued and understood, which increases their commitment and loyalty to the team's objectives. This mutual respect and trust are pivotal in overcoming obstacles and finding solutions to complex challenges.

One of my favorite examples of positive leadership comes from the movie "We Were Soldiers". Mel Gibson's character is a leader who truly understands what it means to lead from the front. He determines that no matter what happens, he, as the leader, will always be the first to put

on the ground in the battle field. He will always be the last to
. The character fully understands that this type of leadership might
ost him his life. But as the leader, he sees it as his responsibility to care
for his team in this way.

May we all become the "Lt. Col. Hal Moore" of our own teams. May
we all be the first to pick up a challenge, and the last to seek personal
comfort or safety. May we all be unwilling to step away from our
workplace complexities until every last member of our team is safely
carried to triumph. May we all remember that leadership is not about
us. It's about the people who make up our creative teams.

Summary

It's my sincere hope that you enjoyed taking this creative leadership
journey with me. As we conclude, let us remember that the journey
of leadership is continuous and ever-evolving. Each day presents new
opportunities to learn and grow alongside our teams. The stories we've
shared, the principles we've discussed, and the examples we've
considered are but stepping stones on a much larger path.

So, as you step forward from this exploration, carry with you the
understanding that leadership is not just about directing or delegating,
but about inspiring and empowering. It's about making those around
you feel capable and prepared to face whatever comes their ways.
Through this approach, we not only achieve remarkable outcomes but
also contribute to the growth and fulfillment of every individual within
our team.

Thank you for joining me on this exploration of leadership. May your
path be marked by curiosity, passion, and unwavering commitment to
those you lead. Together, let's continue to push the boundaries of what
our creative teams can achieve.

About the Author

K. Lee Butler is a versatile writer with a passion for crafting insightful and engaging content. Known for her expertise in nonfiction how-to's, she offers practical guidance on topics such as communications, content design, and creative living. Her work has helped individuals and businesses improve their writing, storytelling, and overall communication skills.

Beyond her nonfiction endeavors, K. Lee also explores the realm of fiction, indulging in the mystery genre.

Residing in southern Virginia with her husband, Brandon, K. Lee draws inspiration from her personal experiences and surroundings. Her unique blend of creativity and knowledge makes her a sought-after author in both the nonfiction and fiction worlds.